BRIGHTER THAN WHITE
An Autobiography

On 15th November 2003, Gladys Wontner-Riches died from pneumonia, after having fractured her ankle in a fall. She was eighty-nine.

This is her story, in her own words, set against the backdrop of the Great Depression, two World Wars and the austere days of postwar England.

Born Gladys Elsie Wontner in 1914, her childhood was spent in the oppressive shadow of a mentally unbalanced mother, whose unremitting coldness, and at times vicious cruelty led, one dreadful night, to Gladys and her sister Betty fleeing from their home.

In 1936 Gladys married Rob Riches, but it wasn't long before she realised she was in a strict and loveless marriage.

Many times she would have to make heart-wrenching decisions and face the agony of heartbreaks and false hopes, but she struggled on, driven by an overriding desire for her children to be happy and secure, and for them to have the love she had been denied.

BRIGHTER THAN WHITE
An Autobiography

Gladys Wontner-Riches

ARTHUR H. STOCKWELL LTD.
Torrs Park   Ilfracombe   Devon
Established 1898
www.ahstockwell.co.uk

British Library Cataloguing-in-Publication Data.
A catalogue record for this book is available
from the British Library.

Arthur H. Stockwell Ltd. bears no responsibility
for the accuracy of events recorded in this book.

Acknowledgements

In grateful thanks to the wonderful doctors and nurses who operated or looked after me at Torbay and Brixham Hospitals in the years from 1983 to 2003. In particular, my thanks go to Mr Cline, Mr Pullan and Dr Jowitt.

ISBN 978-0-7223-3847-6
Printed in Great Britain by
Arthur H. Stockwell Ltd.
Torrs Park Ilfracombe
Devon

PREFACE

Around the age of twelve, my mother began to tell me about her childhood. The stories she told me about her young life were disturbing, as it was clear that she had had a very unhappy upbringing from a mentally unbalanced mother. She impressed upon me that, although her life had been made to appear worthless by her mother, of all the awful punishments she was given, none were as bad as those handed out to her younger and very close sister, Betty. Some of the punishments given to Betty were inhuman, and my mother does not include all of these in her autobiography.

In or about 1960, my mother began to write down her childhood memories. Only very slowly did she put them to paper, as in 1963 my father bought a grocer's shop in Fleet, Hampshire, and the writing stopped for another thirty-five years.

On 12th August 1998, my mother had a major operation in Torbay Hospital. She was in Allerton Ward, and the 'red team' prepared her for her operation that afternoon. Mr Pullan carried out the operation, an ileostomy, which removed the whole of her bowel. The operation was successful, but around midnight her blood pressure plummeted, and she was taken immediately into Intensive Care.

At one o'clock a.m., the phone rang and I was advised to come straight to the hospital. I rang my father and told him the grave news and that I would come round right away to pick him up. We drove to Torbay Hospital deep in thought, but on the way I said I had had bad feelings about this operation ever since Mum had taken the decision to have it. We parked immediately in front of the main entrance and got the lift up to Allerton Ward. The night orderly met us and guided us down through private hospital areas to Intensive Care. We rang the bell and a nurse ushered us into a waiting room, telling us that we could not see my mother just yet, as they were still trying to stabilise her.

A good hour passed by before a doctor came in, saying that she was now in a stable condition, but not out of danger. He had concerns that her bladder was not passing water, but we could go in and sit with her.

The Intensive Care room was dimly lit, and we found my mother with a number of tubes connected to her, as well as an oxygen mask covering her nose and mouth. The nurse tried to allay our worries, and found chairs for us to sit on. Dad sat with a concerned expression, whilst I hovered anxiously around her bed checking her monitors. Every now and then the nurse returned to do her own checks. We sat through the night by her side, till around 5.30 a.m. I noticed urine appearing in the bag below the bed. I immediately told the nurse, who smiled and said, "Good. She will be all right now," adding, "why don't you go home now and get some sleep. Phone us later to find out how she is."

We drove home tired, but very relieved that Mum was OK. It was getting light when I dropped Dad off. I then drove on to my house. I managed a half-hour sleep and at 8.00 a.m. I phoned Intensive Care. I was told she was fine and would be transferred back to Allerton Ward sometime in the afternoon.

Later that afternoon, my father and I were in Allerton Ward when my mother was wheeled back into her empty space in the ward. Her surgeon, Mr Pullan, arrived promptly and shook hands with both of us. He told us that her operation itself was a complete success and that her sudden relapse had been unexpected. However, he thought that she would make a full recovery.

My mother was still very much under the effects of the anaesthetic and drugs given her, as the red team set about their duties in looking after Mum and making her comfortable.

The next day, Friday, my father was admitted into Crombie Ward, which was immediately underneath Allerton, for a hernia repair job. So, late that afternoon, I arrived to visit both my mother and my father.

I found my mother sitting up in bed, with some colour in her cheeks. One or two attachments had been disconnected, but the saline drip and tube to her stomach were still in place. I kissed and embraced her, but said nothing about the worrying time that Dad and I had gone through. When I went down to see how my father was, I was held back from seeing him, with a nurse telling me he was still in 'post-operative state'. "Come back tomorrow to see him," she said. They didn't allow me near his bed, but I looked down the ward and saw a couple of medics attending to him.

I went back up to Mum and told her, and said I would see her tomorrow.

Next day, Saturday, I found Dad in bed, a sick tray lay beside him. He looked pale. A nurse pulled me to one side and told me that my father had had a suspected heart attack during his hernia operation. I sat with Dad and he wanted to know how Mum was. I told him that she was fine and had been sitting up in bed. Then he was sick again and the nurse came and took the tray away, leaving a clean one on the bed. When I went up to see Mum, I found that she also had been sick. Not wanting to worry Mum, I didn't tell her what the nurse had told me about Dad.

For the next four days, I got to the hospital around midday to visit both my parents. My mother was slowly regaining her strength, but my father remained bed-tied with a drip attached to him now. On Tuesday, my father was transferred to a heart-specialist ward. He said he was thirsty, so I went and got him some blackcurrant cordial. When I visited him next day, where his bed had been was an empty space. I panicked and looked around, but no one was there to speak to. I went out into the corridor, just as Dad's empty bed was being wheeled back to the ward. A nurse told me he had been taken to Intensive Care, but there was nothing to worry about.

At 10.10 a.m. next day the phone rang, and a voice told me my father was dead and my mother had been informed! I was shocked and fell to my knees in the hall.

My head was in a spin as I drove to Torbay, going straight up to Intensive Care. A foul-mouthed family were sitting in, on, and around the floor outside, showing no signs of respect in such a worrying area. It was the last thing I needed. I rang the bell and eventually a nurse came. I said I wanted to see my father. She took me to him. His mouth was wide open. I touched his arm and it was still warm. I stood and looked at him and was then taken into the office where a bag of his personal possessions was handed to me.

I went straight up to my mother in Allerton Ward and we hugged each other. The ward emptied to give us privacy. "Don't worry, Mum," I said, "I'll look after you."

The 27th August 1998 was the day of my father's funeral, and my mother could not attend it as she was still recovering in hospital. When my mother finally returned home, she was in a subdued state and had problems with her stoma. Her stoma nurse was Brandon Gwilliam, and, after a short return to Torbay, she was transferred to her local Brixham Cottage Hospital. There Brandon visited her. I sat outside on the steps, waiting for him to arrive, which he duly did at 2.45 p.m. accompanied by a female trainee. With tears in my eyes, I voiced my concerns over the deterioration in my mother's health since the operation, by showing him recent photographs of my then happy mother.

Brandon was wonderful to her, and prescribed my mother to smile three times a day. When she was back home, she did try hard to follow his advice, but, despite all I could do for her, she remained in a low state of depression.

One night, as she lay in bed, I tried to offer some advice. I told her if she didn't try to lift her spirits, then nobody would want to see her. I said, "Do you remember back at Ruislip you started to write your autobiography – why don't you have a go at finishing it?"

The next morning, so my mother later told me, her depression had lifted, and for the next few weeks and months she continued writing and completing her own unique life story. Many times she would wake during the night, turn on her bedside lamp, and continue writing it.

She was resolute that it should be called *Brighter than White*, for reasons only she knew. I have done my very best to make her autobiography as easy to read as possible, without losing the style in which she wrote it.

In the early morning of 15th November 2003, my mother, aged 89, died from pneumonia, after having fractured her right ankle in a fall at home, in her bathroom.

I had now lost a most dear and precious mother, and I was now, more than ever, determined that her story would be published, no matter how difficult it might prove to be or how much it cost. Her last years were happy ones. She enjoyed life and her love of nature right to the last.

Michael Wontner-Riches

"Look forward and not back,
Look out and not in,
And lend a hand."

CHAPTER ONE

As I commence this unusual story of my life, my son is sixty-one and my two daughters, born out of wedlock, are fifty-three and fifty-two.

My childhood and teenage years until my marriage in 1936, aged twenty-two, was exceptional and, for the main important part, very unhappy.

I was born on 19th March 1914, five months before World War I, or The Great War, as it was called. My parents rented a terraced house in Mellows Road, No. 26, and it was very easily recognised because it had a step down to the pavement. The front doorstep was kept white from daily hearth-stone and in the windows hung white net curtains. I was called Gladys Elsie Wontner.

Our family name is listed in *Burke's Landed Gentry*. It is of ancient origin and derives from the Manor of Wentnor, Salop. It is mentioned in the Doomsday Book. Wentnor is situated between Shrewsbury in Salop, and Leominster in Herefordshire – two centres with which the Wontner family were associated for many centuries. It was from the Leominster branch of the family that we were descended, when the young sons of John Wontner, namely John and his younger brother Thomas, set off to seek their fortunes in London shortly after the death, on 8th July 1761, of their grandfather Thomas who was the proprietor of the Golden Lion Inn, and they established successful businesses in watchmaking and the law.

My two sisters, Betty and Joyce, were born in 1915 and 1921 respectively. We lived at Wallington in Surrey.

I remember Grandpa John Wontner as a very gentle and quiet man. He was a commercial traveller for a stationery firm, walking and bussing his rounds. He carried a large attaché case with him. Grandma Wontner was very tiny. She had a gentle tone always. Her hair was white and parted in the middle. She and Grandpa lived at Mitcham, Surrey, in a terraced house. There was a large cherry tree at the bottom of the garden, which was Grandpa's pride and joy. He had planted the cherry stone there himself, many years ago, behind the latched gate where the path led you through to Aunty Mary's house (my father's sister). He also had an elder brother called William Hoff Wontner. Dad was born last in 1886, late in his parents' marriage, and he was adored by his mother.

The house of Aunty Mary, Uncle Ben and little Benny was an untidy home. Whenever we visited them all, my mother never came. Betty and I played with Benny in Grandpa's garden. Grandma would be cooking Sunday dinner on the black oven-and-fire range. Once she gave us hot apple tart with lovely crisp pastry. Betty, who did not always travel well, was very sick going home. Mother was extremely cross and said Grandma knew we would be having our own dinner upon our return and Dad should have known better and stopped us eating it.

Aunty Mary was sharp in voice and manner, Uncle Ben quiet, and Benny very mischievous. He showed us how to wet without knickers – always a mystery for many years. Dad's brother William (Uncle Will) was married to Margaret Hannah Dixon (Aunty Maggie). He was very smart, legs in breeches, whilst Aunty was fat and ugly but very kind.

When I was nine, I passed my first piano test for the LRAM, and Dad took me to play for Grandpa and Grandma. Their piano had keys missing, but they seemed pleased with the pieces I played for them. I had a Bible sent from them, a special colour-illustrated one. The frontispiece showed Jesus holding a lantern with the words 'I am the light of the world.'

Dad told me that Uncle Will had lost his first girlfriend, who was both beautiful and slender. She jilted him and he told Dad that he would go out and find an ugly fat wife whom no one would want. They were an odd pair. They had no family but befriended two nurses and gave them both a home. These two nurses lived with them all their lives and nursed them to both their deaths. Uncle had a lovely organ, which he played well. At his death, he

10

bequeathed it to his local church. He was a member of the Plymouth Brethren and he preached regularly. The nurses (Aunts I called them) baked cakes every Friday to give to the 'Poor Sunday Tea' held weekly in their church hall.

Uncle cycled over to see us quite often. With his breeches he would wear a very smart flat cap. He would take me on his knee and tell me he had invented a saucepan which was divided up to cook different things on one gas ring. Mother told Uncle Will off afterwards for filling my head with such rubbish! She disliked all of Dad's family, so none of them visited us. Later only Grandpa, after Grandma had died at the age of seventy-seven, would come over to us for dinner. He had a beard, and, fascinated, we watched him eating then wiping it with his crisp white serviette. He smoked a pipe, and I was sent to buy the tobacco with a shilling. The tobacco was 11½d and I could keep the halfpenny change.

Grandpa always brought us three girls a packet of Palm toffee, which he would put in his trouser pocket before journeying over to us. So it was always soft and sticky when he arrived. Mother would take it away from us always. He told Betty and me stories – always the same! He had, he said, a wonderful thing to put on his fire – he didn't need a sweep. It went up the chimney in flames. Mother said he talked rubbish!

Two of his jokes I remember. A preacher stood in front of his class for a prayer, and said, "And the Lord said unto Jesus . . . Sit down, my boy, sit down." Then he would ask us to spell Constantinople. As we got to Constanti, he would say "No." After a few times of trying, he would burst out laughing.

Aunty Mary and family moved to Portslade in Sussex and Grandpa went with them, so we didn't see him again.

My father was exempt from war service as he had a blocked left ventricle of his heart, which was hereditary. My son has the same condition and was exempt from his national service.

By this time none of my father's family visited us – Mother rowed with them all. We never saw Aunty Mary's family again. My father read of her death in the obituary column of the *Daily Telegraph*, and told us some years later.

My earliest memories are from my cot, crying, and Mother and Father coming upstairs to me. Father stood in front of the wardrobe glass door, and his inside rumbled. I asked what that was and Mother said it was Daddy's supper and cocoa. I remember I used to have bad twitches in my legs when waking up.

Our house was very clean. Mother would do the washing on Mondays, shutting Betty and me in the dining room and I remember being smacked for drawing on the steamy window. Mother's washing was very white, her hearth and steps too. They told you that all of Mother's home was like that. She always impressed on us the fact that she was a very good mother and that we owed our health – in fact our lives – to her care and that we ought to be very grateful. Unfortunately for us, she was not a loving and cuddly one. She was so very cold and forbidding that, as I grew older and began to know other children and compare their mothers with mine, I often felt of little worth and that lots of given love must be wonderful. Her strictness never wavered with my sister Betty, some eighteen months younger than myself, or with me.

Living with us during those war years was my mother's sister, Aunty May. Just fourteen years older than myself, she was, I remember, a happy carefree girl, but she was subjected to the same strictness and order as ourselves. She constantly rebelled, resulting in many rows and tears. I adored her, and used to creep into her little box-room bedroom and sit with her. When the weather was warm and sunny, she would sit under the syringa tree, while she wrote letters to her brother, Nunkie Vic, who was 'in the trenches' in France, and I would write scribble for her to pop in the envelope. Sometimes she would crochet, and try and teach me with a crochet hook and a penny ball of rainbow wool. She played the piano beautifully and sang, but this was often at night under our bedroom. I used to toss and turn and finally scream, only to be soundly smacked by Mother, so I did not exactly appreciate her talent. Usually the next night, Aunty May would pop into my room with some little gift – a leaf carefully peeled to reveal a delicate network of veins – a 'skelington', as I called it – and other such small surprises.

At the sound of aeroplanes, we were taken downstairs and put under the dining-room table, with Mother and Father sitting in the big basket chairs, which creaked and cracked at every move. One night, when it was thought a Zeppelin was near, we all lined up along the coal-cellar wall, whilst Father made 'cinnamon milk' to prevent us from catching a cold.

Suddenly one day, everyone was outside and calling over back fences, and the word 'armistice' was used over and over again. My mother was ill in bed, due to eating boiled rhubarb leaves, so nothing especially exciting took place in our home, though I remember my father putting a very faded Union Jack out of the window, with the flags of several other countries too.

At the age of six I started school, at the Misses Meedmore. This was a private school in an old house, organised by old Mrs Meedmore, and the pupils were taught by her two daughters. After a seemingly endless first day, with four very long walks, Mother was in tears, and a long discussion took place in the evening with Father. I didn't really understand what it was all about, but next day Dad took me to school soon after eight o'clock, and I was taken into an empty classroom smelling of polish and disinfectant. I was introduced to 'the boarder', who I thought must be connected with the blackboard in some way, and we played tiddlywinks until school started.

At dinner time, I was taken down to the basement with one or two of the other girls and given the worst-tasting dinner I had ever had. The greens were yellow, and you could have made bricks out of the squares of rice pudding. However, life went on at school, and each morning my father would take me, then run like mad to the station to catch his train for London. On the way to school, he would buy me a penny sponge cake at the little baker's shop, which I thought must always be open, as it was so early in the day.

Mother gave us a very plain and uninteresting diet on the whole, and she had very definite views on what was good and bad for children. We were used to seeing her eat cheese, fancy cakes and other quite ordinary things, making no protest at our usual plain bread and butter. At school girls and boys often brought sweets and fruit that we had never seen before, but we were absolutely scared to ever accept them, lest a tummy upset would reveal our sins. One thing always took my eye though – humbugs! Big fat brown and yellow humbugs! I used to drag at Dad's arm and beg, "Can't I buy one – just once?"

His answer was always the same: "Your mother says no."

As those of the 1919 era will remember, potatoes were very scarce during and just after the war. I used to be sent with a green string bag to the tiny greengrocer's on the other side of the road past the shop which displayed my beloved humbugs. I couldn't explain just how I found the courage to provoke my mother's anger, but I turned away from the greengrocer's, went into the humbug shop, and popped three humbugs into the string bag. I returned home with my new-found strength fast dwindling, and, as Mother answered my knock on the door, I gasped, "Mr Sparkes hasn't any potatoes, so I bought some humbugs."

Mother used to keep the cane alongside the tea tray on the meal table, and we always accepted the fact that we needed it. I can't remember feeling rebellious, except on one occasion, and I think I resented it all my early childhood, when I thought of it.

Mother was proud of her garden, which she used to tell everyone she did alone, because Father had a bad heart. So of course we had sufficient warnings and promises of just what we should expect if we dared pick any of her flowers.

One morning, Mother got up to find that several of her geraniums had been broken. The previous night we had been playing on the grass by them before going to bed. Betty and I were brought before Nunkie Vic, now demobbed and out of work, and duly questioned by Mother. Betty's denial was accepted, but Mother said I was such a little liar, bringing up the humbugs in support of her statement. I burst into tears and, remembering that Aunty May had said God could see you even through green blinds, said loudly, "God knows I didn't, and he was looking." Mother thereupon seized me, pulled down my knickers (to my utter humiliation in front of Nunkie), caned me soundly and sent me to bed. I remember my father coming upstairs and without saying much, sat by my bed.

Some time later that day, Mrs Challon, the lady next door, popped her head over the fence and said she was so sorry that her cat had had a fight in our garden, but she could see that fortunately only a few blooms were broken. Hoping for some sort of compensation – perhaps even a humbug – I waited until bedtime and ventured, "I had the cane for nothing, didn't I?"

Mother's face never softened. She snuffed out the candle and said, "That will do for all the other things you have done."

The neighbours on either side of us were elderly. Mrs Challon had an invalid daughter, Maggie, who seemed like a shadow. She used to glide about, very pale and very quiet. They were very poor, but very proud, and every spring she would say, "We have been planning the carpets and curtains; Maggie thinks the blue would look better with the gold curtains this year," or words to that effect. Mother would say it was empty swank and she didn't believe they had any carpets at all.

On the other side lived a little old lady named Mrs Gear, who would peep through a knothole in the fence by our back door and talk to Mother. On washing days, her pink wrinkled fingers used to poke through with a sweet for each of us, which Mother would promptly put on the copper fire, saying you never knew where she got them from. Eventually Mother had a row with each neighbour in turn, and they never spoke to us again.

One afternoon we found our back way soaking wet on a dry day, so Mother filled a bucket full of water, and, going to the upstairs back window, waited until Mrs Gear came out of her back door and poured it all over her! Later that week the landlord called and gave my father notice to quit, which he ignored, and we continued to live there.

When I was seven, Mother seemed to develop into a 'well invalid'. Things in bottles stood in the larder 'for Mother'. Father said, "She isn't well." She looked all right to Betty and me, and we wondered what all the fuss and mystery was.

One morning I woke up to hear moans, and they came from Mother's room. Then I heard a funny kind of squealing and the sound of Mother sobbing. Presently Father came in to get us up, as he usually did, and he said, "You have got a new sister" – that was all.

We had just got over whooping cough, and were not at school, so we went out into the garden. It was June and boiling hot. "We don't want the little beggar – what a nuisance she will be!" I said. However, we were curious to see her, but it was a few days before we were allowed to quickly peep.

Mother said, "You have germs and you don't want her to die, do you?"

I don't think either of us were quite sure about this, but despite the fears she lived. She was a real stranger in our eyes, for, unlike ourselves (both fair-haired and blue-eyed), she had our father's colouring, dark hair and eyes like currants.

By this time Betty had joined me at Miss Meedmore's; and when we returned after our whooping cough, it was decided that I was old enough to take her, on my own. Poor Betty had not completely conquered her bladder, and was forever being found in a 'pool'. One morning I did not feel well and cried bitterly, begging to be allowed to stay at home, but Mother put on her coat and, with the baby in the pram, marched us the good mile to school. I cried all the way and Betty cried in sympathy.

Miss Meedmore was sympathetic, and we were just in time to join in the prayers and hymn. Suddenly one of the children said loudly, "Oh, look – the River Wandle," and there stood Betty in the usual pool. At this, I started to cry again, and so did Betty. Eventually one of the 'big girls' was commissioned to take us back home. She took us to the corner of our road and left us, and we ran crying rowdily to hammer on Mother's door, causing people to come and enquire what had happened.

When Joyce, our new sister, was a few months old, Aunty May and later Nunkie Vic left us and we never saw them again until in adulthood.

My father's brother, Uncle Will, would come on rare occasions and take me on his knee, but one day there was a big quarrel and we never saw him again until many years later, when he took my father and I out in his new Morris Cowley. That was the last time we ever saw him. From that time on we became sufficient unto ourselves, never going anywhere, except school, and a walk in front of our parents on Sundays. Mother told us that we had no need of friends, as we had each other to play with and people only wanted to find out all your business if they came in. Thus we accepted her opinion and regarded everyone with caution and suspicion.

Father seemed to be very remote and disinterested. He was kind enough – indeed, we ran to him with all our requests – but I never remember him ever kissing us; nor did he ever suggest anything or give any opinion on our behalf to Mother. She reigned supreme in everything that went on in our home.

Betty was a plump and curly-haired child, but very chesty and delicate. I was very thin and quite straight-haired. We had our hair plaited and scragged back from our faces, but on Sundays we were allowed to have it loose, crimped from the plaits at the ends, and with a bow on top. We wore frilly white cap-sleeved overalls, always, indoors.

By the time Joyce was a year old, Betty had developed what Mother called tantrums, and she became a sulky and defiant child. Somehow I never had any spirit of defiance towards Mother. I was inclined to be cowardly and one stroke of the cane cured any attempt at disobedience. I used to wish that Betty would give up her tempers, as it was so much easier to give in, I always thought.

When we went to and from Miss Meedmore's, we always took a

certain route on Mother's instructions, although there were at least three other roads we could have taken. One of the boys lived in the road we took, and one day he jumped out on us, both arms outstretched, and sang out that he wouldn't let us past. We were so afraid that we both started crying, and, when we eventually reached home, told Mother that the little boy in green was going to stop us going down his road and please could we go down the next one. The usual answer came: "Certainly not – and no arguments!"

Next day we confided our terrible fears to a girl who lived in the next road to the little boy in green, and said that Mother would never know if we went down her road home. It seemed an easy enough way out, so we went with her after school, skipping and running, which was an unladylike thing to do and forbidden by the school. Suddenly I tripped from a playful push by the bigger girl, and as I rose, blood poured from my nose. The girl's mother took me in and, after pouring cold water over my head and face, said it was just a 'cut on the nose'.

I arrived home red-eyed and red-nosed, whereupon Mother gave me one look, rushed me upstairs and into bed, covering up the mirrors on the wardrobe and dressing table, telling me not to dare to get out of bed. I don't know how long I lay there, or how she ever got our doctor, for there were no telephones nearby, but he arrived and, after looking at me, went into consultation with Mother. I heard him say, "Stitches will show badly; I think we will try plaster." My nose was encased from top to bottom with a plaster cap, and over this two strips across each cheek. Both eyes went quite black.

I was off school for some time; but still with the plaster on my nose, I returned with a note for Miss Meedmore. I had had several taunts from my classmates already – 'Old Plaster Face' and 'Boss Eyes', so I felt sure Miss Meedmore would sympathise. As I stood before her, she said to the class in general, "This is a naughty girl who disobeyed her mother and went home the way her mother had forbidden," and I sat down red-faced with shame. It was the first time that Miss Meedmore had spoken to me in a vexed tone.

However, this was soon forgotten and all was obviously forgiven too, as old Mrs Meedmore asked me one day if Betty and I had a doll's pram, and if not, perhaps we could ask our mother if she would like us to have one. With the necessary permission given, we were both taken into the basement and shown a pram, newly painted white. Miss Meedmore said that it was once Miss Ethel's and that we must not tell the other children about it; and we were sent home half an hour earlier, out through the back entrance. We were thrilled and took turns to push it home.

We always had our set tasks to carry out from as early as I can remember. There was silver and brass to clean and knives to polish on a board, upon which we sprinkled Oakey Powder, then we put the knives into grooves along the edge of the board to polish the edges.

One Saturday it had rained very heavily, and we were then sent out to the shops. Betty carried the string bag and the half a crown, whilst I pushed the pram with Joyce in it. Just where the road curved, a large muddy pool had formed and bright-red creeper leaves were floating on top. We had been crayoning creeper leaves at school, and Betty loved drawing and painting. I let go of the pram and we both bent down to pick out the prettiest, when, accidentally, the half a crown in Betty's hand fell plop into the water and disappeared into the drain. At the same time the pram rolled silently backwards and, before we could stop it, toppled over the kerb and fell upside down with Joyce screaming and covered in mud. My mind flew to Mother's oft-repeated warnings: "Be sure your sins will find you out," though I wasn't quite sure if this was sinning. Mother soon decided for us, and we received the caning anticipated.

Sometimes caning was accompanied by the additional punishment of bed, at any hour of the day. I remember the feeling of triumph when I got upstairs once to find the bed unmade. Another punishment was to have to stand in the bath with the water running to 'drown naughty girls'!

As Joyce grew up, we felt an even greater resentment towards her, for Mother used to kiss her, and she made it quite clear to Betty and me that she was a good child, and that we were not. I cannot say that we were unduly unhappy, except for childish disappointment when apparently ordinary requests were always refused. Betty and I had each other and there were always compensations. We took to pretending and inventing a great deal. Half a banana, wrapped round in a hankie and kept to suck noisily in front of the other children, was an ice cream. Mother said ice cream froze in your stomach. We also ate pretend sweets, rolling our tongues into our cheeks.

CHAPTER TWO

When I was eight, I went on my own one day to a larger school, and I sat for an examination. When the summer holidays were over, I was dressed in new clothes and given a string bag with house shoes, and in my pocket a buttonhook for my outdoor boots. I entered the big entrance hall unseen amongst the hustle and bustle. Going up to the same peg in the cloakroom opposite the entrance, where I had been told to hang my hat and coat for the entrance examination, I hung them up, unbuttoned my boots and put on the new house shoes. I proceeded to wander among the girls – all very big and grown up – until a bell was rung, and everybody disappeared except me.

Suddenly a grey-haired, statue-like lady came gliding along the passage, a black gown flowing behind her. "And where are you going?" she asked sternly.

Later I learned that she was the headmistress, Miss Katherine Irene Wallace.

"I don't know," I replied.

She took me to a small room where a smiling lady sat behind a typewriter. "This is Miss Moon; she will look after you," and the grey statue glided out.

I learned afterwards that Miss Moon was the school matron, and that any girl could knock on her door with any aches or accidents, after having been given permission by her form mistress.

She took me outside the building, across the playground, out by a large gate, across the road to a little church hall and into a largish room where another grey-haired, tall and unsmiling lady, Miss Cuthbertson, stood before a class of girls of my own age.

The morning passed quickly and it was soon time to go home to dinner. All the class disappeared into a cloakroom and I followed them in, expecting by a miracle to see my hat, coat and boots there. Soon the cloakroom emptied and I was in tears. Miss Cuthbertson hurried me back across the road and back to Miss Moon. She questioned me very kindly, and I could only say, "It was a cloakroom." As the school went round in a square, all the passages between looked alike to me. It took a great deal of asking other girls and searching before my clothes were found. Left to myself, I found I was quite unable to button up my boots. I had never done it before. I remember I cried a great deal, and that a big girl eventually came and did them up for me. That was my first day at Wallington County School for Girls.

Here I soon became very unhappy, and the early days remained a horror for me. I was taunted by the other girls over my button boots, and finally shunned because I never spoke. I was an easy target for pranks – my buttonhook used to disappear with regularity, and I begged Mother to let me have shoes like the other girls, but she said boots were to strengthen the ankles and give me good straight legs.

(At Miss Meedmore's we had all been very happy. Both the Misses Meedmore were kind and softly spoken, and they were not old.)

Very soon I learned that two girls dominated the playtime and 'before bell' assembly. You were either on Joan or Mary's side! The first time a girl spoke to me was to ask "Whose side are you on?"

After some discussion with the two girls, neither of whom wanted my membership, Joan said resignedly, "Oh well, she had better be on my side, I suppose."

It soon became very plain that the coveted side was Mary's, and that her side was privileged to annoy and badger Joan's side.

By this time I had developed a bad stutter, and this became the butt for much amusement. Joan used to stand me on a chair and demand that I repeat sentences, everyone shrieking with laughter.

Each month, there used to be a sort of bring-and-buy sale, in aid of the 'orphans'. We were asked to bring any cakes or sweets, which were laid out on the seats of the front chairs, and some money to buy them with. Mother refused both requests point-blank; she had 'never heard of such a thing'.

I remember looking at the various objects, not especially longing for any of them, except some green nuts which were like some

Father had once had in a wicker box, only Father's were brown. They were frilly round the tops. They were marked '4 for 1d'. One of the girls asked if I was buying. I replied that I had no money. She opened her hand, in which she had a pile of pennies, and gave me one.

I had never dared to eat anything strange before, but I went straight to the girl who was 'saleslady', and pointed to the nuts. Four green nuts went into my tunic pocket, and I tussled with my fears, the possible poisoning and punishment, but I dug my teeth into the shell and extracted the kernel. It didn't have any particular taste, but I finally ate all four. All day I expected to feel very ill, or even perhaps die, though I didn't know what the latter disaster was exactly. Nothing happened, but my terrible sin lay very heavy inside. It was the first time I had been deliberately deceitful, and it occupied all my thoughts for a very long time.

I don't remember anything about the actual lessons. I used to sit with my finger in my mouth and think about other things. Miss Cuthbertson used to say, "Take that finger out of your mouth. We must buy you a dummy," and a little titter used to ripple among the girls.

One afternoon I lifted my desk lid at the commencement of lessons to find a yellow and white jelly dummy inside on the pencil ledge. I found out later that it was from the girl who had given me the penny. Her mother kept a sweet shop. I had thought that she was friendly, but not now.

But there was something in which I found happiness at last. I began to have piano lessons, and the singing mistress found I had a voice. It was nice to be asked to stand up and sing alone, because I was a dunce at most things, especially sums. The piano lessons were given by Miss Hewitt, in a room in the first building across the road. I was given a time to go to her, but I was unable to tell the time. Miss Cuthbertson showed me where the hands would be on the clock, using the blackboard pointer to reach the clock. I looked up and down with the regularity of a Mandarin, until she relented and said she would let me know when to go.

Miss Hewitt was a pale, expressionless lady. She had tight gold 'earphones' over each ear, and her hair was parted severely from front to back of her head. Her waxy-looking fingers wore white mittens, and she was sitting on the right-hand side of a piano in a narrow little room. She showed me middle C and how to touch that key with the ball of the middle finger. Next she explained the beat, using ta, ta-a, or ta-a-a for crotchet, quaver and semiquaver. My 'practice' was to tap out on middle C one line of crotchets and quavers with ta and ta-a accordingly under each, and then the same crotchets and quavers under which was written 'Lit-tle Bo-Peep has lost her sheep'.

Every morning before breakfast and after tea, I was shut in the front room for practice. If it was cold, I wore my outdoor coat, and Mother would say, "I want to hear that piano played for half an hour, and you will sit in there until I say you can come out."

By some quite unexpected ability I progressed and soon passed my first examination.

Next year, my class was over in the converted houses opposite the main building. The mistress, Mrs Newton, was a smiling, kind and gentle lady. Her voice was almost musical. I never remember her ever being cross, and the year with her was the happiest of all my schooldays. Most of my old class had come up with me, but most of them now left me alone, to my relief.

One of the new girls, a big fair-haired girl spoke to me several times at playtime. We discovered that we lived near each other, so we went home together. She suggested that she might come and call for me next morning, but I was horrified at the thought of it. "Mother would be very cross if you did," I said.

She replied, "All right, you call for me," which I did. So began a friendship that is still cherished by me today. Her name was Margarite Janes and she too had a little sister.

We came home one afternoon a little earlier than normal. Margie seemed to understand the importance of keeping to Mother's rules, and we never dawdled or stopped at her house to talk. This afternoon, however, she said, "Would you like to come and see our tennis court?" so I followed her into her garden.

It was mostly grass-covered, with one big herbaceous bed on one side. The tennis court was on the other side, whilst at the end of the garden were some trees, under which hung a swing. Presently her father came through the garden gate wearing tennis flannels and carrying a tennis racquet. Margie picked up a racquet and soon they were hitting the balls and laughing. It had never occurred to me that fathers ever played with their children; it seemed almost odd. I asked her, as I left, if her father always played with her and she replied, "Of course – always."

So life became fairly happy for me, though I still stammered badly, even to Margie. She never seemed to notice.

Mrs Newton taught us many things besides the three Rs. She explained the right and wrong things to do if we wanted to be thought ladylike. To list them here would be impossible, for they are too numerous, but they have remained with me always. She had a way of making us want to please her – it wasn't any effort to try hard to do our best. She encouraged everything we did, always saying gently, "Not quite right, dear; I should try again." She also tried hard to teach us to speak nicely, repeating 'the ohld ghold common' and similar phrases.

Mrs Newton was most interested in my music examination success, and, after I had been with her some weeks, said that as I had such a nice voice, perhaps my mother would allow me to enter the local Festival of Music competition. Mother seemed pleased about this, as Mrs Newton would give me a half-hour lesson after school, in her own free time and for no fee.

I learned in later years that she was a widow with two young children, and I wish I could have thanked her. Instead I took it quite for granted. However, I won several medals and certificates, and I expect that was the only reward she looked for.

When I had been in Mrs Newton's class a term, my sister Betty left the Misses Meedmore's and came to my school.

Miss Cuthbertson had died, which did not surprise me, as she was white-haired and very wrinkled. The class was now taken in the old house opposite by a young but very ugly woman, with a fringe and straight hair and a pasty and deeply pockmarked face. Betty said she was 'all right' and she seemed to settle in very well. I was a lot happier now; I loved Mrs Newton and I had my sister with me once again. One or two of the girls spoke to me about her with interest, and when one of them met us out with Joyce, she became quite friendly. I was proud to boast to the enemy that she didn't have any sisters like I did.

If we fell down, or caught cold or were sick, Mother always said it was our own fault. I never remember a word of comfort or sympathy from her. Her remedies were harsh and crude to say the least: witch hazel, syrup of figs, yellow flowers of sulphur, and treacle were handed out, applied or swallowed.

As soon as Betty had come to the County School, we stayed to dinner, because Mother said she could take Joyce out more. The dinners always had a peculiar smell, and my memories of them are chiefly haricot beans and stew, and hard-baked treacle tart. After we had finished our dinner, some of us used to carry the dirty plates back to the kitchen. One day I fell down and smashed some of the crockery and cut my finger rather deeply on the knuckle. I can remember screaming and being taken to Miss Moon. She bathed the hand and bandaged it and was very kind and soft-spoken.

When I still stood there, she told me to go back into the playground.

"What will my punishment be?" I asked, terrified.

"You won't be punished, dear," she said, "you can't help accidents."

I couldn't believe my ears. No one had ever spoken to me like that before. There was no need to invent any reason for my bandaged hand to anyone, and, what was more, my fear of Mother's anger and the replacement of the plates was at once dissolved. She need not know, and she never did. I told her that I fell over and no more.

The following years took on a more normal pattern. I passed a music examination each year, and sang and played with both Mrs Newton's and Miss Hewitt's help and encouragement. Sadly, however, I was a complete dunce at arithmetic, and in Form III just couldn't understand any of it. I used to struggle so hard, and longed to have ticks and not crosses in my exercise book. However, Miss Chivers was never cross with me – in fact, she was a very placid and gentle little woman.

One day we had a form test of decimal sums. They were written up on the blackboard with the decimal points in various positions. I copied them down and suddenly had an idea. The answers would be chalked up on the blackboard at the end of the test, so I made some pretence of counting with my fingers and looking up at the ceiling. At the end of the test, I hastily copied the answers and handed in the work for the desired ticks and ten out of ten marks given.

Miss Chivers asked me to stand up, and then, with a stern look I had never seen before, said, "To be a dunce is shameful, but to cheat is wicked. Stay behind and I will see you after school."

I was not allowed to go out to play, or play games for a week. The experience absolutely cured me – I never cheated again. The bit of respect I had so coveted from my former enemies now stood in jeopardy, and I could have died with shame. Margie was brief in her comment: "It was a silly thing to do. What does it matter if you can't do arithmetic?" and she never referred to it again.

When Betty was ten, she contracted pneumonia. The winter was very severe, and we were snowed up for weeks. As I now came out of school later than Betty, we each went home on our own. One night Betty started shivering in bed, and I couldn't get to sleep. I told her to stop and that made her cry.

Mother came in and told us both off. The next morning Betty couldn't get up, and after a few days she got worse, so a doctor was called. Within our house, there was a sombre and quiet atmosphere with whisperings between Mother and Father.

By now Betty was in a coma, and Mother made me sleep with Father, which I hated. "Betty has always been delicate," Mother used to say, when referring to her; but I was horrified when an ambulance arrived and she was taken away to hospital. Mother told me she might die, because her lungs couldn't breathe.

Then followed the frequent visits to the hospital with clean clothes; whilst for me, I had to walk around Purley in the hard, bumpy and downtrodden snow with Joyce, during the hour's visit. We were not even allowed to wait inside the entrance, and I never knew if it was Mother or the hospital who forbade it. Betty was operated on and recovered sufficiently to return home. I came back from the school prize-giving one January day, and she was there, in a sort of bed-chair. She was like a skeleton, her lovely curly hair was cut off, and I burst into tears.

"She mustn't stand up yet," Mother said.

"Oh no," I said, "of course not. Her legs would break, wouldn't they?"

The old family pushchair was brought out, and, when the weather turned warmer, I used to push her around in it. She was away from school for a whole year and I missed her terribly.

A new school had been built much further away from our present one and this was yet another obstacle for me to overcome alone. This was the first 'big' building I had ever been in. It had so many rooms and corridors that for the first few days I was too terrified to ask to be 'excused', because it meant first finding the lavatory, and then finding my way back to where the classroom was.

Each morning we had assembly in the big hall, before marching along the corridors and up the stairs to our room. The rooms all looked alike to me, and I could not find any distinctive landmark to bear in mind. Our class had been split up now into A1 and A2. I was in Lower A1 and to my great sorrow Margie went into Lower A2. However, we still met and went home together, and I soon got over that.

The new school was beautiful, with different rooms for all the special subjects taught. The highlights were the art and the chemistry rooms. The art room had individual easels with low lights over them. I really wished I could draw and paint; but the gift was not mine, although I tried really hard. Betty had the gift, though, and spent most of her convalescence painting. Father had some of her paintings bound into a book and it was sent to the hospital for the children.

We had moved now and were living in a bungalow at 1 Link Lane, Wallington. It was named Sandy End and was built by a family friend. Its layout was planned by my father, and it was the most uncomfortable home I have ever lived in. If you sat in the dining room, you had the draughts from all of the bedrooms, the drawing room and the hall, all blowing over your feet even in the summertime. The dining room had two doors facing each other on opposite sides of the fireplace, so that in the winter we had an ugly screen to sit behind, and then we would have to push it into the corner before we could open the door into the hall. With five of us in the family, there were many comings and goings through the doorways. Only the person who sat in the crook of the screen and beside the fire kept warm. That was Mother's chair, and in this bungalow, for nine years, she sat in it and ruled us all. We all lived in awe and fear of her, and especially Father. She would be sitting in it when he returned from the city and he always kissed her cheek and handed her the paper.

He was a dark-haired and swarthy-cheeked little man. His eyebrows were black and he wore a black pinstriped suit and bowler hat. Sometimes we took our scooters up to the station to meet his train. One evening we met him halfway and I said that if he wasn't my father, I'd be afraid of him, he was so 'black all over'.

As we got into our teens, we used to creep out of our bungalow very early in the morning and go for scooter rides, sometimes before seven o'clock. Mother never got up early. Father took her tea, and, as far back as I can remember, dressed us when we were small and got our breakfast. In later years we got our own and Father's, and left for school with Mother still in bed.

On these early morning rides in the early twenties, we used to see queues of children outside the baker's, and coming out again with sacks on their shoulders. We were very curious, and asked Father what they were doing. He told us they were getting stale bread and cakes and he didn't think we had better go out so early in future, as people might think we were doing the same.

As the school was now a long distance away, I was given a penny for the tram if it was raining. Margie had a bicycle and I begged Mother for one, as Betty was still at home a year after her illness. Margie had taught me to ride hers and we used to walk and ride in turns coming home.

To my great joy a brand new Raleigh bike was brought home, and a whole new world was opened up for me.

On school half-days, Margie and I would cycle to Banstead Downs or Epsom Downs. In spring we would look for flowers, in autumn for nuts and blackberries.

Once a lady gave Margie a large crisp apple because she took back her cat that she found lying in the gutter outside her house. As soon as we were out of sight, Margie cut it in half by banging it on a sharp stone and we cycled off happily chewing it.

Another time Margie found a two-shilling piece. Next day she handed me a shilling. I protested that she had found it, but she said, "We were both cycling along that lane, and so we both share anything we find."

I have never forgotten that, and the pleasure that shilling gave me.

CHAPTER THREE

The school and Margie became my life from the age of twelve. My home and my parents I avoided as much as possible, as it was too miserable for words, with everlasting rows. I can see, looking back now, that some of the trouble was my mother's determination to be in the 'upper class', sending Betty and myself to fee-paying schools for purely snobbish reasons. Neither my father or my mother ever attended school functions open to parents, or were present on prize-giving days, for although we were not poor people, it was always a financial struggle for my father.

School reports were a misery to me. I tried hard but I just wasn't an all-round academic child. Some subjects, like English, English grammar, spelling and French, I was able to get high or even top marks for, but for most other subjects only fair, and maths always poor.

"She could do better, but will not concentrate," was a typical comment.

Only one teacher was observant enough to realise there was something more on my mind at times – the memory of some awful upset at home, or the fear of going home. My problems were many and I had no one to confide in at all – not even Margie. I had to pretend that my home and my parents were the same as other girls' and I used to invent exciting visits to aunts. But we never visited anyone and no one ever came into our home. Margie called for me and waited on the doorstep, but never complained.

Coming home from school was timed to the minute. "Come straight home," was called out daily by Mother; but if Margie and I really hurried, I was able to go into her house for a few wonderful moments to see her pretty bedroom, or speak to her mother.

Once I remember her father coming in. He was full of fun and Margie suggested, "If we are quick, we can get a set of tennis in

28

with Daddy against both of us." Greatly daring, I went out into the garden and onto the tennis court. Their mongrel dog, Jummy, was told to sit and stay by Margie's father and I thought she was the luckiest girl in the world.

I flew home afterwards with a picture of it all in my mind that has never left me. I can see the garden, Jummy, Margie and her bespectacled father as though it happened yesterday.

Invitations used to come from various girls and their parents to tea parties in their gardens and this was always a double worry for me. Firstly, plucking up courage to ask permission to go, because Mother always knew some sinister reason why I shouldn't – they were unhealthy, or a bad influence, or she 'knew all about them'! The other dread was saying I couldn't come and then being asked why.

My feeling of inferiority was strengthened as each year passed, and if I hadn't had Margie as a friend, I cannot imagine what life would have been like for me.

A year after the new school opened, Betty returned. Joyce remained at home and seemed quite happy as Mother was always kind to her.

Our school mistresses were varied in age, all single and mostly stern and hard-faced, also two widows, Mrs Chase-Brown and the kindly Mrs Newton.

Deportment was strict and seniors watched over our conduct and reported unladylike behaviour.

The school I have already partly described, and its solid building and beautiful grounds were slowly giving me a solid background that I could trust and enjoy. Our school motto was 'Self-Knowledge, Self-Reverence and Self-Control'. It was on our cap badges (green woolly caps that came right down over our ears), our blazer pockets and in summer on the hatbands of our panama hats.

School uniforms had to be bought at just one outfitter's shop near the school, and Betty and I were always conscious of our faded caps and blazers, and Mother complaining bitterly at the cost.

One day the headmistress took us both aside and said she had a letter for our parents for us to take home.

In it she politely pointed out that our uniform was rather shabby and below the standard she liked to see.

My mother was furious and sent us back with her reply.

Miss Walters read it, and then eyed us sternly, saying something about school governors would be told, and we must come to school dressed properly and that she could not have 'shebby gels'.

Miss Walters was the grey-haired lady who floated past me on my first day and who took me to Miss Moon. She was stern-faced and tall, and on the few occasions I stood on the carpet in front of her desk in her study I was terrified.

If we were absent, a note had to be given to her, and one time I had been at home with a cold.

She read the note and said, "So you have had a cold in the head?"

"Oh no, Miss Walters" I replied, "it was only in my nose."

"And where is your nose, child?" came the same stern voice. I could just see a glimmer of amusement on her face – the first and only one I ever saw.

But stern as she was, I remember my fear of her lessened. On the platform of the assembly hall each day she said prayers. One came up so many times it became so real and so inspiring, I have made it my own favourite. There was no doubt it gave me the firmest foundation and a store of wisdom to fall back upon all my life.

It was Philippians, Chapter 4, Verse 8:

> Finally, brethren, whatsoever things are true,
> Whatsoever things are honourable,
> Whatsoever things are just,
> Whatsoever things are pure,
> Whatsoever things are lovely,
> Whatsoever things are of good report,
> If there be any virtue, and if there be any praise,
> Think on these things.

It was July 1928. We broke up with the usual fun – six weeks' summer holiday ahead.

We had had holidays at Shoreham, Sussex in recent years, renting beach bungalows from Mrs Wise. She lived in a large long house at the end of the Widewater, an inland stretch of water, grass-edged and -pathed, made by a huge sea swell years ago. Mrs Wise's house was on a very large plot of land in Kings Drive, with a right of way between the house and garden leading to the main Portsmouth road.

We never saw a Mr Wise. We were told he lived at Thakeham on their large farm.

There was a pretty, very blonde, very thin girl, Eileen, there. She was the same age as myself. She worked very hard, rowing up the

Widewater with boxes of vegetables and flowers from their garden for all the tenants. She fed the chicken and did errands for many daughters of Mrs Wise, who lived in railway shacks – very attractive – in the Old Fort Road. I remember Aunty Flo, Aunty Do, Aunty Ro and several others. Eileen was adopted and during summer lived at Shoreham, and at Thakeham in the winter working on their farm.

Mrs Wise was old, dressed in black, and slept in the afternoon. Eileen had to stay in, keep quiet and do mending or other silent tasks. Betty and I befriended Eileen, and Mrs Wise allowed us to join Eileen, and to play tennis and go into their beautiful gardens. These were tended by a gardener and had wide grass paths between large vegetable beds. I remember the scent of the rose beds. In the winter I would write to Eileen and a friendship formed, which lasted from 1928 until 1995 at her death.

Eileen met her real mother one day every year – a Mrs Randall. She married her cousin by adoption and had two sons. We went yearly to Shoreham, and Eileen grew into a lovely girl.

In July 1928, after school break-up, there were rows and tears at home and we were eventually told that our 'hut' at the bottom of the garden was going to Shoreham, to be built on for holidays.

Father contacted a man on Old Salts Farm who owned small plots by the Widewater. All along the banks buildings sprang up, and there was a towpath to a bridge to get to the beach.

We always had a hired car with a roof rack which carried our two large trunks with us five packed inside the car for the long drive from Wallington to Shoreham. Father paid £1 for this.

We were driven to a plot on the Portsmouth road, where the hut and nothing else stood. This hut was big – solid – with a large locker. At home, we were sent to it to play and keep out of Mother's way. The locker kept our toys etc.

Mother started crying. Dad said men would come and add to it. He went back to London, assuring Mother that men should have erected rooms on the main shed, and he said he would call at Old Salts Farm on the way to the station.

We all slept on the floor close to each other. Drinks were made on an oil stove and all we ate were biscuits that first night. It was late August and mercifully the night was warm.

I can't remember next day, except it was warm and sunny and all three of us were sent up to the beach. When we eventually returned, we found two men there and Mother crying bitterly. The men said we must comfort Mother and be good. Later, we walked back to the beach worried and very upset about it. We had had a good upbringing in a comfortable home – this was all so strange.

The month of August ended. Dad came down and said we had to leave, as the plot was sold, and we must go to Mrs Wise to stay. Betty and I stayed in her house, whilst Mother, Dad and Joyce slept in a large shed in the garden, sleeping on a mattress. Daily, Betty and I would go down to the shed and have our breakfast and cup of tea.

It was now September. I asked about school, and Dad said we wouldn't be going back just yet – he hoped it would be soon, after a governors' meeting.

Eventually we returned to Sandy End and the weather turned cold in October. That winter was very hard and I got chilblains badly for the first time.

Life at home was unhappy, with Mother continuously shouting and rowing. She took to saying she was going to leave and telling me that I would have to look after things. She would go off out at night, whilst Dad would sit and clean all the cutlery with powder, very quietly.

All of us slept in one bedroom, Betty and I in a double bed, and Joyce in a small bed which rattled when she moved.

One night there was a loud bang on our front door. Police had found Mother wandering in the middle of the road!

Next day Father told me Betty and I couldn't go back to the County School. I was fourteen and, being the eldest, must do Mother's work, as she was ill. Betty was twelve and Joyce seven.

I was plunged into washing, cooking and shopping. Mother either sat in her chair or stayed in bed. When in bed she would choose who would see to her, as she thought the others would poison her tea or food.

Somehow life went on like this for a long time. Then Mother began to live life differently. She bought, or rather ordered, expensive made-to-measure costumes and clothes. She also dealt with nurserymen in the Stafford Road, ordering plants and rustic work. She spent hours in the garden and often wouldn't come in for dinner.

Betty was my critic. She would eat her meal, banging on the underside of the table and say, "A bit hard, but its all right!"

We did daily shopping for the four of us. Dad ate in London, and just had tea and breakfast with us. I remember buying, daily, two pounds of potatoes, a cabbage and fruit, mostly apples, and in

Doick's the baker's, a cottage loaf, before going on to Liptons to buy a quarter-pound of patted butter. Loose tea was ordered and delivered regularly from Croydon.

As we were growing up quite fast now, Mother cultivated the garden, enabling us to bottle fruit and make jam. She ordered two greenhouses, one for growing cucumbers, which was kept closed to retain the moisture, and one for tomatoes, where she grew Ailsa Craig. We were allowed to weed in the garden.

Life was a little more normal now. Over the high clinker front wall Mother would speak to people and tell them, "We keep our daughters and they have no need to go out to work."

Always, in between, Mother's face would suddenly change into a frightening one and find a reason to shout at us. Betty would say, "Look out, Mother's got her horrid face." She would refuse to obey her and say, "I shan't" or "I won't" and when threatened she would say she didn't care what Mother did. This led to beatings and locking her out all day, which was very upsetting. Betty had a determined spirit and she would say later, "I had lovely food out there," and smack her lips. "You are a coward," she would say to me.

I was. I hated being hit and would try to please Mother, which mostly was useless. These moods lasted until Dad came home. Then he was told he must 'see to Betty'. Dad's nature was quiet, but he would get up and push Betty to bed for punishment.

Mother never went out for two years and Dad developed nervous asthma. He was up all night, sick and ill, yet kept on travelling up to London to work. At night he would walk home from Wallington Station reading the *Evening News*.

As we grew up, clothes wouldn't fit and underclothes and woollen stockings were darned weekly. My navy reefer from school lasted for years. It was short and of unfashionable length. One day I was sent to the dyers and cleaners with two of Mother's coats, to be dyed dark brown. These were for Betty and me, and looked awful to my eyes, but at least they were warm.

We became very frugal, and one morning a man knocked on the door. My father looked terrified, but after discussion the man went away. He was from the council. Dad wrote articles on law, and life, and persuaded the man that a cheque was due.

At this time, I had no idea of our circumstances regarding money. It was in the mid-thirties that my father and family were plunged into dire straits. More of this later.

CHAPTER FOUR

Dad worked as a solicitor's managing clerk for Millar and Sons and earned £6 15s a week. Mother took £3 15s, and Dad had fares, lunches and all the bills to pay with the remainder. In these years £2 a week kept families of road workers and general workers. Their children went to council schools. So Dad's money was good, augmented by money from the weekly articles he wrote for the *Passing Show*, *Weekly Telegraph*, and *The Cyclist*, and short stories for the *Evening Star*. Law with humour were the main themes.

But Dad owed money from way back. He had allowed Mother's whims and spending to reduce us all to extreme poverty. Mother spent her money happily on the latest crazes, and constantly rowed because she wanted more. Dad was afraid of Mother and let her spend.

We lived on cheap food – I cooked breasts of lamb, stews from offcuts and 6d tins of corned beef, with only one loaf a day to share between the five of us, and never cake! We were all very thin, except Mother. She had food kept in her bedroom – chocolate biscuits and sweets.

We never queried her demand for special things. She was Mother, and we always accepted anything to keep her quiet and normal.

Our outlet from our dreary existence was our daily walk through Roundshaw Way, which was cut to allow traffic from the Croydon Airport to Purley. You could see the airport with its hangars and tall wire fencing surrounding it. Along the Way there was a spinney, which gave us pleasure in its seasons. We were told that the large mushrooms we found there were horse mushrooms.

We invented a club. Each of us had a name: I was Hannah Porky, Betty was Minty Rhino, and I forget Joyce's. I kept the notebook, where our poems and items of interest were entered once a week, whilst lying in bed.

We all went to bed at 7.30 p.m., until Betty and I were allowed to stay up later. Betty was a born comic. She gave people names and made up poems about them. I remember very few of these, but they were always very witty. We made nature notes, never entering any of our domestic cares and worries. So quietly did we hold our 'meeting', whispering and laughing very softly so that any of our bedroom noise was fortunately insulated by the heavy screen inside the dining-room door.

Our opening 'song' was always:

> Half a half a dozen in a circle,
> Making a drefful awful din.
> Can't make such noise 'cause Pater
> Is prowling in the dark.
> Suppose we wake up Mater –
> Oh, ain't it an awful lark?
>
> The cats outside are howling,
> Alpenrose is in his bed.
> And if a ghost comes prowling,
> Perhaps we'll wake up dead!

We always woke up well alive, if a bit tired, and had much satisfaction from our Tuesday secret. Our notes and club book we kept under the lino edge by the fireplace.

Betty continued to annoy Mother, and defiantly took all the punishment with Mother cutting up her skirt. Betty would sit and cobble it together and say loudly:

> "No cake for you, my girl –
> You haven't cleaned your teeth.
> When you're in your coffin,
> I'll not buy you one wreath."

This sort of gibe would cause things to be thrown up in a rage. I remember Mother hurling a milk jug at us, with all the milk going everywhere.

I still used to see Margie sometimes. She had made another friend, and told me that she now went to the Crusaders on Sundays. She asked if I would come and see if I liked it.

Mother said, "No!" but surprisingly my father said, "Why not let her?"

I had no hat and still wore my navy reefer coat. Dad took me to Croydon on the tram, and bought me a deep-green hat, which I loved. However, I didn't like the Crusaders, and so instead went to the Presbyterian Church Sunday School and settled happily there.

After Sunday dinner, I would wash up (soda in the water) with Betty drying. Then I would walk along Stafford Road to the crossroads of Stafford and Manor Roads, and join the cheerful superintendent and class teachers. I was in the senior class, and after hymns and prayers our class went into the vestry and were given a talk by Mr Hopper, who during the week was a bank manager. One talk by the superintendent I remember well. It was a story about a boy on a train and how he met a man who was a broad Scot, who told the boy, "Jesus furast, oothers next and yeeselves last."

Every Easter and in the summer, Mr and Mrs Hopper gave us wonderful treats. At Easter, we were taken to a tea room where we were served lovely cakes and given an Easter egg. In summer we were given an afternoon trip out in the country and a tea. I remember one occasion clearly when we went by train to Leatherhead on a lovely sunny day. Mr Hopper wore plus fours and brought his shaggy dog with him.

We started the walk at Box Hill and walked across Ranmore Common to buy our tea. I fell in love with Ranmore; it was a haven of wonder – birds and insects everywhere. We had photographs taken, and had a very nice tea served on outside wooden tables. Afterwards we walked on to Dorking Station, tired and happy – all twelve of us.

Mr Hopper's family were grown up, and I thought that the magic of wealth was the reward he used for his and Mrs Hopper's contentment.

Betty came with me later. We wore brown coats and often Mother's size-4½ shoes, which crippled us. I took size 5, but we kept going. Later I became the pianist at Sunday school and Betty kept accounts and affairs. After the meetings we walked home with a tall, dark and gentle teacher. For years she lived in Carew Road with her parents. I loved her deeply, and got her interested in my newly found charity work. Mother was completely disinterested in our doings, so long as the housework was done. After breakfast, I would stand on the corner of Stafford Road and collect for the blind and other good causes. Mother said I couldn't bring any boxes back home, as people would talk! I would stand with my box until it was collected off me, then make haste to go home to get the dinner. I remember the blind charity gave red rosettes.

Later on, local fêtes attracted Betty and me. We used penny packets of crêpe paper to decorate my bicycle, winding it all round the spokes of the wheels. We dressed up in old clothes. I was Little Bo-Peep and wore a long pink nightdress and sun bonnet, whilst Betty was Little Boy Blue and had a short tunic made from a blouse, bare legs with boots. We enjoyed our parts and collected a lot of pennies. We never joined in with the stalls in the park until we were older, being shy, but happy, after doing our bit, to go home.

Neither parent was interested in these activities, but for us both they were a carefree diversion from home. We never worried over Joyce at all – she never said much and we felt she was too young to include.

On bank holidays we planned to do 'something special' – usually a long walk. One I particularly remember in August: it rained non-stop, but we walked all the way to Epsom Downs.

Arriving there, we saw a huge board with 'Douggie Never Owes' on it, and we wondered to whom he never owed? We walked the paths, ate our bread and cheese and drank our bottle of water, before returning home in our rubber-backed raincoats. The rubber was rotten on our shoulders, so we got wet, but the freedom and sight of country and houses gave us memorable pleasure.

We lived among what we called the 'upper classes', and neighbours only sometimes spoke to us. We regarded them with fear and suspicion.

Alpenrose lived next door to us, a man named Cyril Coward and his wife. They were kind and tried to invite us round. I asked Mother. "Certainly not – no children of their own, and trying to borrow mine. You are not to speak to them." Later Mother would tell us they had thrown snails onto our lawn. Mr Coward was an artist who drew and wrote a weekly article for the *Sunday Express*. His studio was in a garage at the bottom of his back garden.

Betty invented names for everyone – she said we could talk about them outside, and no one would know. There was Mr and Mrs

Private-Means, Mr Never-Went-to-Work and Binkie White (a man with very blond hair). These are just a few that I remember.

One day I thought I would learn the deaf-and-dumb sign language I had read about, then teach Betty so we could talk to one another without Mother understanding. It was quite easy. I saw by luck in a magazine an illustration of the whole deaf-and-dumb alphabet. I can still do the alphabet and also 'Our Father who art in Heaven'.

Sunday school was the highlight of the week. We also were able to join in evening events, such as concerts, where I sang and played the piano and also recited poems. Betty helped with scene-shifting, or being one of the shadows, made behind a sheet doing hand patterns.

We never went to any of the morning church services. However, there were 'silver services' where our blind organist played hymns, and prayers were said. You took silver coins to put in the collecting box, and we would ask Daddy for sixpence to take with us.

I have a lovely memory going back to childhood, when Aunty May took us to Beddington Church one Christmas morning in the frost and cold. We had been given muffs, and Aunty let us hold a toy inside them. The church had a lychgate that was decorated with green leaves and flowers and we sang carols happily and joyfully.

When I was sixteen, my father gave us pocket money. I was given 2/6d because I worked in the house, Betty had 1/6d and Joyce 1/-. I used to save my money, as 10/- bought hats or some fur for the collar of my reefer coat so as to be in fashion. A 2d fare took us to Croydon on the tram, where we would wander around Kennards store in the high street. Outside the cinemas we would look at the placards in wonder, as we had never been taken to see a film.

At Wallington we had what people called the Flea Pit, and one day Betty and I went to see *All Quiet on the Western Front*, which was being advertised everywhere. So one Saturday afternoon we told Mother that we were going to look round the local shops for a change. The cinema was smelly and dark and the film horrified us, but we sat through it. When eventually we left, we looked up at the clock above Morgan, Baines & Clark's Estate Agents and found it said six o'clock. We ran the good mile home, expecting to find a very cross mother. When we arrived home very breathless, we found our clock only showing ten past five. What a relief! 'Morgan Baines' had set their clock an hour forward, as it was summertime at midnight that night, and they closed on Saturdays at 1 p.m.

Things at home were getting much harder. Mother didn't seem to give us much money for food, and it was harder to do the shopping with what we were given, and eat as we once did. No bacon-and-egg breakfast for us any more!

> 'Over the fence leapt Sunny Jim,
> Force is the stuff that raises him'

– so the packet read on the table. Father always made the tea and ate bread, and left before eight o'clock to catch his train to London. He had a long walk to the station. I disliked Force, but we ate it with milk and sugar on it. After washing up and bed-making, shopping was next.

We had new people in the greengrocer's shop at the bottom of our road – a man and his plump wife and a younger man who did most of the window display and delivered orders on his bicycle.

I went daily to the shop for two pounds of King Edwards, some carrots and onions and sometimes greens, because we grew sprouts and savoys in our garden.

I liked the boy – he seemed too well spoken and smart to be in this job, and we had polite talk and laughs. He always took girls I knew out for walks. He wore wide Oxford bags, brown-and-white Manhattan shoes and his hair shone with Brylcreem. He had a sort of swagger and an important manner about him.

Behind the greengrocer's shop was an alleyway with a garage opening out onto it. We could look out on it from our back window. The boy, Rob, used to come out with an airgun and try to shoot sparrows on the roof next door. I said to Betty, "Look at that swanky boy. I wouldn't go out with him if he asked me."

One day a man called and saw Mother. He was a school officer, and he said Betty and I must go to the council school and complete our education. Mother flatly refused the suggestion, and said Joyce, now eight, was taught by her – this was untrue, but she could read and write a little.

Eventually Father put me into the Conservatoire of Music to complete my exams and achieve my LRAM diploma. Betty was taught violin at the same place. She got on so well that she joined the local orchestra and played second violin for a performance. But art was her real gift, so Father put her into the Surrey Arts and Handicraft Society. She had two pictures chosen for exhibition.

One was of Queen Elizabeth I with her courtiers, drawn in black and white at the Whitgift school in North End, Croydon. She sat daily in a shop doorway opposite the school copying the huge iron gates. The other was a watercolour painting of a fable, the story of which I now forget.

I passed the higher music exams well, then found I had to do the next two quickly without sufficient time for aural work. My tutor was Langford Guest, kind, but firm. I hated his smell. I found out later it was the Harris-tweed jacket he always wore.

Between my housework, I had to practise for three hours daily, often in a very cold north drawing room. I was born with poor circulation, from having very narrow veins, and my hands were often stiff with cold.

I used to pass Coles Fruit Shop, music case in hand at eight o'clock at night for concerts and music meetings in the Guests' own home, and often saw Rob still working in the shop. This was in 1931 and 1932.

One day Rob stopped me and said, "Would you care to come for a stroll with me?" Very flattered, despite my previous opinion of him, I said, "I don't mind," and we met next day after the shop closed – about 8 p.m. I was told by my parents to be in at nine o'clock.

After several walks, Rob said other girls stayed out later, and that he was a chap who liked a change anyway. I was deeply offended, yet I liked him, but we finished our walks and chats. He told me he had lost his mother when he was nine, and had led his own life since. "No one tells me what to do," he boasted, standing legs astride and looking straight at me.

I carried on with my life as it was. I always had Sundays to plan for, with piano introductory music whilst the children took their seats. Our senior class had about ten girls now, and we always met at half-time in the vestry, with Mr Hopper's stories from the Bible chapters.

One Sunday, he gave us a week's competition. We had to memorise all the book names of the Old and New Testaments. That was no problem to me – I had learned long poems easily at school and could recite easily. So next Sunday I won his prize without hesitation. I can still remember most of the Old Testament to this day.

Some months after Rob told me our meetings were finished, there was a fête held at the Beddington Orphanage, and Betty and I sold programmes at the gates. At six o'clock entrance was free, so we had tea with friends, leaving our boxes (now heavy) in the tent for helpers' use.

About 8.30 p.m. we met Rob with George Welford, one of the local boys I knew. We all four went to the roundabouts and swings. Betty and I had never gone on any of the pleasure-ride sections of the fêtes and carnivals we helped at, but I agreed to the roundabout and sat on a horse. It was awful, to me, when it gathered speed, but I clung on hard. Rob came to help me off and asked if I would be his girl for good. I asked him why he was putting the question to me for the third time? He said he had come to the conclusion that eight girls out of ten were no good, and there were only two worth knowing. Really surprised and flattered by this disclosure, I said yes.

The next day, Sunday, I asked my father if I could go out later with Rob and told him proudly what Rob had said. My father smiled and said he would ask Mother. He didn't mind ten o'clock, but said I should ask Rob who the other one is?

I started a happy life with Rob; however, Sundays were Presbyterian weekly dates, so I asked Rob to come. He refused point-blank and said he would go out with the boys.

I told Mr Hopper that I had a boyfriend and must give up being a pianist because I was afraid of losing Rob. Mr Hopper said I must bring Rob to tea with Mrs Hopper and himself. It was summer, and I wore a cotton dress; Rob was in Oxford bags and pointed shoes. Mrs Hopper had baked cakes and was very kind. Neither mentioned Sunday school, but Rob was definite that I should leave, so I did. I was seventeen. Betty carried on for a time, keeping their book and notes.

Sunday outings were happy – long hikes in the Surrey countryside, and meetings with Rob's friends in their homes playing games. I was taught billiards and played well, as I had a good eye. Always I had to be home by ten o'clock, and Rob used to go back after.

The conditions at home were hard. We were poor, and Betty and I fitted in badly with charity events. Our clothes were awful. I bought some material at 1/- a yard, and hand-sewed a 'Mabs Fashion' in tissue silk, with honesty-seeds pattern. It had a big bow at the neck, and I felt very smart. Poor Betty, though, looked well washed and mended. She had lovely hair, curly and blonde.

One awful week we had our gas and water cut off – Father hadn't paid the bills. Mother used a wooden stick to turn the water on at night. Cooking was done on two oil stoves. I don't know how we lived through these times – we just existed.

My last year at the Conservatoire saw three exams. Two I passed, but the third I failed and Father said he couldn't keep Betty and me there. I let all my piano practice drop and rarely played at all.

Food was a problem for all of us. Meat was alternately two breasts of lamb (3d each) or a tin of corned beef (6d). Stews were some scrag-end of beef, half a Symington's oxtail cube, salt and pepper. One loaf was cut up into thin slices to share. We were very well, though very thin.

When I was nineteen, I said I would get a job. Mother didn't refuse, and I found a job at a paper-and-sweet shop in Manor Road. The woman owner was business to her boots. She said I must give a reference. Mr Hopper gave one immediately. He told me later that he knew of our problems. My father had been to him and asked for a loan to pay the gas, and he had refused. I was horrified and very ashamed, but I never told Father I knew.

The shop hours were 7.45 a.m. until 7 p.m. The first hour I wore a brown coat and cleaned the front outside, then the shop floor, before finally dusting everywhere. At 8.30 Mrs Walton went upstairs to have breakfast, whilst I put on a white coat and served papers and cigarettes to the people on their way to the station. Player's cigarettes were 11½d for twenty, Afrikander tobacco 1/- an ounce. Small white-tipped cigarettes, De Reszke Minors, were in oval tins, thirty for 1/-. Most people bought tobacco in one form or another. Workmen would buy Player's Weights, ten for 2d. It was said they were swept up from the factory floor. It was non-stop selling. At 8.45 Mr Walton came for his paper, and then went to London on the train. He worked in textiles, and always called Mrs Walton 'Betty, old girl'. They were in their fifties and had no family.

My wage was 18/6d weekly, entered in a book. This was left on the counter one day, and I looked in it. I saw the last assistant got £1 a week, so I asked why I only got 18/6d. Mrs Walton was very cross and told me it was a private book, which I had no business to open. She said I had no experience in shop work.

She was very brisk in her manner and called the shop front 'the winders', which I cleaned and dressed with plates of sweets, with the counter opposite. Mrs Walton said I could eat sweets, which I thought was wonderful, but I soon grew to dislike them. My only loves were fruit-filled jellies. These were in rows in boxes, so there was not much chance to take one until you served someone with them. Terry's All Gold chocolates were 5/- a box, Cadbury's big bars of chocolate were 2d. Betty and I ate very few as we got older, but I did enjoy all the pleasure from the smells and the nice people who came in the shop to buy.

Rob and I played tennis in fine weather, and went to the pictures every week, enabling me to escape the many rows still going on at home. Betty told me about them. She now did all the cooking, and I would cycle home for dinner at one o'clock. "You may go, Miss Wontner," would be announced. At night, often there would be no customers, but Mrs Walton would wait until the clock said seven o'clock on the dot, and again would say, "You may go, Miss Wontner."

The Walton household above the shop was large with two storeys, and run by a girl of fourteen, called Eunice Griffiths. She was from a mining village in South Wales. Her father was a miner. I was sent upstairs occasionally with a message, and Eunice would be in the big kitchen with an iron range, warm and cosy. Her hands were red from hard work, but she was proud to be able to send money home for her family. I told her that my money was also keeping regular food in our household. I kept 2/6d for myself.

Sometimes Mrs Walton sent me out to collect unpaid paper bills, often from large houses. I liked the fresh air and the variation from my shop work. One place, I remember, was a lovely home where I was invited in by a servant. The lounge smelt of cigarettes, and on a settee was an open chocolate box with a lot taken out. I sat and waited until, eventually, a lady came in yawning and said she had got up especially to see me. She told me her husband saw to paper bills and things like that. I saw *London Illustrated* on a table and thought they must be very rich and forgetful.

At another house lived a lady JP who gave me the money and asked me about myself. I was afraid to talk much, but she told me to come and see her again anytime. I never saw her again, but I used to wonder why life for so many people was so calm and peaceful, when my own home was so awful with constant rowing and now so untidy and dusty. Betty was not a born housekeeper and would return to her drawing and painting whenever Mother

43

was out of sight or she had a free moment. All the chairs had papers and odds and ends on them. Mother moaned, "No one puts things away." She spent her time in the conservatory and garden. The front was a picture: laburnum all along the wall, with the flowers linked in bloom. People would stand outside and gaze at it. Our wrought-iron gate, made at a local foundry, had, at the top of it, three hearts and the name Sandy End. Our road, Link Lane, was between Sandy Lane and Redford Avenue.

After my work, I went out with Rob. When it rained we went into the cab of the lorry, which was kept garaged down the alley behind the shop. Rob said he would come and ask Mother if he could call me his girl and take me to dances and bring me home a bit later sometimes.

Mother grabbed me inside and said, "Certainly not," and "She isn't your girl."

In the hall I cried and said, "I love Rob."

She replied, "You don't know what love is at nineteen. Look at him – lad of the village in his pointed-toed shoes."

I ignored her, and Rob and I continued to meet, parting just around the corner, to be home at 10 p.m. I told Mother that I was at various musical meetings, and all was well.

After knowing Rob for two years, one night he said his employers, the Coles, were visiting relations in Fulham, and he took me into the back door of the shop. It smelt of stale greens. He handed me some grapes, from a barrel of sawdust.

It was winter and we went up into the flat above the shop. It was a small room with a sink and a cooker in it. There was a fireplace which was flickering and dying, also some chairs and a table. Then he showed me his bedroom. It was tiny – just a bed and a chest. The bed was unmade and it all looked very scruffy. I saw fluff and dust and I was shocked. I vowed then to look after this boy properly one day. He was so much more above rough-living, as he kept his clothes smart, soaking his flannels in petrol in the backyard before pressing them.

We played tennis weekly in Mellows Park. Afterwards, we walked down the hill to the sweet shop and had a ginger beer. We went by tram to Waddon, where Rob belonged to a club for all sports, run by a firm who made slot machines. Rob was in the semi-final of their tennis tournament, but once again had to get me home by 10 p.m. before returning to the sports club to continue his match.

Rob's employers, Charles and Alice Cole, sometimes took us out with their family and friends – all very modern. One of them used to say that I hadn't any powder or lipstick on. I would answer that I used both.

Stanley Cole was the younger brother of Charles, and Rob's best friend. I disliked Stan, he had a nice girlfriend, Eva, but he was a show-off, full of himself and very sarcastic to me.

Joe was Rob's elder brother by six years, and he came one Sunday to Charles and Alice, bringing his girlfriend, also called Gladys. Rob said he would take me to their home next Sunday for the day. Joe worked in London for a catering firm and was allowed to take home food for special occasions. We arrived at midday, and Gladys kissed Rob. I thought that this was very strange, as our family never kissed. Father would give Mother a peck on her forehead as she sat in her chair when he arrived home from work, but that was all.

Joe lodged with Gladys's parents, the Hendersons, who had a crippled son called Phil, aged seventeen. Gladys's mother was grey-haired with a pale complexion. She greeted Rob warmly, then said her inside was bad. The father came in from his shed. He was tall with a cap and waistcoat. Phil was shy and hardly spoke. Joe got the dinner and, as the weather was cold, we spoke of the problems with the garden from frost.

Not long after I had met the parents, both died within months of each other, the father dying at work. Soon Joe and Gladys became engaged. Rob said that Joe had lodged with the Hendersons since he was fifteen, and people would talk unless he and Gladys married. Later, Rob said that his own father would come and see me, so I begged Mother to let him come to Sandy End. She knew by now I was still seeing Rob, and agreed.

Rob's father sat in our drawing room, and I had to play the piano. The step-mother, Marjory, was very much younger and quite tall, always knitting. She made dresses and jumpers. Her knitting was wonderful.

I went with Rob in his father's car, and drove to Ewell, which was just developing, and my prospective father-in-law said he would provide money for us both to take a shop, and we could then get married. It seemed a wonderful plan. Later we visited his large house at Kenton, where he had a maid who lived in. Marjory's sister, Mabel, also lived there and sat by the fire knitting. Rob's father was an agent for the selling of the newly constructed Costain houses.

An advert on a board on the railway stated, 'Costain Houses – Costing Little'. There was another firm called Costin, and Rob's father said that their houses were cheap and of poor construction. Metroland was now fast developing.

One Sunday, Joe came along with us alone, and we all talked about his wedding plans. Marjory told me everyone slept after lunch, and they all did, Rob included. I was totally lost, and sat on the step of their French window and waited for life to resume. I thought they were all very strange.

It was decided I was to be chief bridesmaid and a friend of Gladys was to be the second one. The wedding was to be on 17th December, so velvet was chosen – pale mauve for the bridesmaids and white for Gladys.

I sat for hours the months before, embroidering a large linen tablecloth with flowers in penny silks of every colour for their wedding present. Rob bought them a metal teapot, jug and matching tray.

The wedding day was frosty with thick fog. When I saw Gladys, she was sitting before her dressing-table mirror and said she ought really to have washed her hair, but I thought it looked all right. She wasn't at all excited – quite ordinary and quiet.

Downstairs, a long table was laid with a white cloth, with placings all set side by side.

Rob's father and Marjory, in a grey squirrel coat, arrived along with various other people, whom I didn't know.

After the wedding, a man with a camera on a stand stood shivering outside, saying it was a 'bad day'.

As soon as the food and drinks were finished, Rob's father got up and said that he and Marjory must go. He patted Joe on the back and said, "Keep off the spirits, boy," and left. Joe was twenty-six, Gladys twenty-five and I was nineteen. Rob and I left later, and carried on as usual with our regular meetings.

One Saturday, Rob said he'd like to take me to Brighton the next day.

I asked, "How would we go?"

He replied, "On the iron horse."

I said, "What's that?" and he laughed endlessly.

The train arrived in Brighton at midday, and we walked down to

46

the promenade. Suddenly Rob asked me to wait there, he had to 'see a man about a dog', and he was gone. I wondered who the man was, and became very suspicious and anxious. Upon his return, I asked who the man was, and got another laugh from him, but no explanation!

We had something to eat in the Undercliff café, then went for a ride along the front on the Volks Railway, in cold open carriages. The day was cloudy and chilly and I was glad to get back on the train and go home. It had been nice of Rob to take me, but he didn't know Brighton as I already did from our holidays at Shoreham. Our family often visited Brighton because of its two piers. Mother would fish at the end of them, and Father would sit and read his newspaper. We three girls would watch the stuntman being tied and chained up, then thrown into the sea. He would come up seconds later, freed of all his chains.

Rob bought an AJS motorbike and he loved to take it all apart, then put everything back together again.

I mentioned the bike at home, and instantly Mother said I must never ride on the pillion. Of course, I did. Rob would wheel the bike round into Stafford Road and we would go off into the Surrey countryside. On my first ride, Rob found a road that dipped and rose greatly. He stopped, turned round and said, "Hang on really tight – I'll show you some speed," and, with me clinging tightly to him, he tore up and down this long empty road. I lost my breath and it scared me badly. Rob just laughed, but he never did it again.

We often visited Joe's household on Sundays. Joe and Gladys now lived at Clapham Common in a large ground-floor flat, and we had dinner with them. One night on the way home the bike broke down, and it was well after ten o'clock before Rob fixed it and we were able to move off again. I arrived home very late, but to my relief Betty was sitting up waiting for me. She was a bit cross and went off to bed. I was very cold and shivering; my clothes were not at all suitable for pillion riding.

In the morning, Betty told Mother I'd been late home, so I quickly had to invent a reason. Mother said that was no reason, and she asked what I had been up to. She told me not to do it again as ten o'clock was a proper hour for girls to be back home. She didn't trust Rob, and I was upset because Rob had accepted the ten o'clock rule and went to great lengths to get me home by then. We started going out most nights, both happy to be out and away from our separate home discomforts.

I still did a lot of jobs at home, especially on Sunday mornings. Mother would lie in bed till very late, whilst Father would put different music on the wireless. It was 2LO in those days, but Radio Luxembourg would play all the modern music, so we enjoyed our free-from-Mother morning.

Mother and Father rowed regularly, but one day a really bad rowing session finished with tears all round.

One Saturday soon after, Father came home with a record to play on the gramophone. It was called 'I Wish I Had Never Grown up to Love You', and on the other side there was a song about a beggar. After dinner we asked to hear it and were stunned by the words of the two songs, especially the first side. I only remember part of the beggar's song:

> I was passing by the churchyard in the city
> And I saw a beggar old and grey.
> With his hands outstretched he asked the folks for pity
> And it made me sad to hear him say . . .
> "Will the angels play their harps for me?"

Mother was furious and then very upset. We all kept quiet and I don't think we really understood the full frustrated reasons why Father had been driven into bringing such a record home.

This record was still in the Fullertone gramophone cabinet in 1977, when their bungalow at Peacehaven was sold.

After a year or so, Mrs Walton brought her niece into the shop to replace me, and gave me a week's notice.

One of my customers was Mr Wise, who owned the piano shop. I had known him since I was eight. He would call in for his paper and cigarettes, so I told him I wouldn't be there any more.

To my surprise, he returned to the shop later and offered me a post with him as a 'senior junior', as I was older than his other junior assistants. He said he would pay me £1 a week and I would work in his new shop being built next to Wallington Town Hall. I would work on commission, at 1/- in the pound, selling pianos, radiograms and wirelesses, but I would be third assistant, for when the first and second girls were attending other customers.

I was in heaven! Firstly, the shop was near my home in Stafford Road; secondly, I enjoyed dusting and standing beside Miss Lane, as she sold the sheet music and records; thirdly, I was escaping from bad and worrying conditions at home. Also I ate my shop dinner with happy, normal people around me. I gave half of my wages to Mother, which was all there was for food then. Debts had to be met, and my father, dressed in his shabby black pinstripe, travelled to St Thomas Street to Millar and Sons and into the law courts daily.

Father had started a book on law called *A Guide to Land Registry Practice*. I helped him to read some of the proofs, most of which were incomprehensible to me, but it was printed and published in March 1928, and regularly updated right up to the time he died in November 1968. The book was used all over the world under that title, and after his death it was kept up to date by a member of the Law Society, and thereafter it has been known as *Wontner's Guide to Land Registry Practice*.

Money was due from one of Father's newspaper articles, and he asked me to seek permission to phone the newspaper from the shop. Phone boxes had now been fitted with dials and I was lost. It had been so easy before to hear the operator ask, "Number, please?"

Mr Wise was on our local council and he kindly told me he knew about our debt problems. He congratulated me on my cheerfulness considering the worrying conditions at home. I made the telephone call, and the fee owed to my father was speedily sent.

In the upstairs rooms of the shop, visiting singing teachers took pupils. I can remember 'Trees' being pulled to pieces by warbling students. How true the words 'only God can make a tree'.

Nothing was happening about the Ewell shop, and life went on without further problems for me from Mother. Poor Betty, though, was still at the mercy of Mother and her brainstorms. Joyce was, as Betty and I had long since called her, Mother's Pet. She knew nothing of our daily tribulations.

However, Father was made to send Joyce to school, and Mother chose to send her to Dinorben School, a privately owned girls' high school. As usual, fees were again unpaid, and a further financial crisis descended. Despite that, the owners kept Joyce there and, in her latter years there, they made her a pupil-teacher. She was quiet and behaved well, but I didn't really know my baby sister very well, as she was remote and apart from Betty and me.

Charles and Alice Cole bought, by way of a mortgage, a semi-detached house in Beddington, just off the Brighton road.

Charles always went off early to Covent Garden every morning. When he returned, Rob would help him unload the lorry. Then Charles would go off to the house to decorate it, and also attend auctions to buy furniture for their new home.

A few weeks later, the Cole family and friends gathered for a party and inspection of the house.

Rob had most of the shop to run. His wages were for his living-in, with just 7/6d pocket money. In the 1930s, the average shop pay was £2. Rob's life was a round of window dressing, unloading and laying out the bins. At 10 a.m. he cycled his rounds, created by his own selling power, going to large houses where maids would hand him their daily list. Alice served in the shop, and in the afternoons she either went off shopping in Croydon or attended to office matters, sitting at a desk. She was a pretty, very plump girl, and I remember once being on the top deck of the tram and seeing Alice struggling on with her parcels. I thought how lucky she was to be so rich.

Rob got all the orders up in boxes, then cycled on the heavily loaded trade bike, delivering to the houses, some of which were a good way away.

As Rob and I wanted to get married, he asked his father if he could look for work in Kenton. The dream shop in Ewell remained just a dream. His father agreed, and Rob gave in his notice and left. By then, the Coles already employed a van driver, and another boy to deliver and help in the shop.

My life in the music shop was full of new interests, and the hours were long and happy ones.

Mr Wise had opened his first music shop in Manor Road, close to the station, just before 1914. Then he had to join the army, and Mrs Wise kept it open all through the war. They had no family.

When I first knew Mr Wise, it was in his second shop in Stafford Road, on the corner of Sandy Lane. We could see the back and the side of his shop from our French windows. It had a white balcony at the top of it.

Amy Johnson, the aviator, upon her return from being the first woman to fly solo to Australia, was driven through the cheering crowds and used the balcony to wave to all of them. We watched all of this from our bungalow.

Mr Wise always took girls when aged fourteen, and kept them until they married. The assistant at Stafford Road was aged about thirty, and Mr Wise put me with her to be taught publishers' methods of music-filing and record-ordering etc.

Miss Lane, the assistant, was a very quiet person and ran the shop extremely well. Mr Wise called in for tea at 4 p.m. in the back room, carrying all his business papers with him. I worked about six months there, before joining the two girls at the new shop.

This new building was large, with only one floor, and it had been designed by Mr Wise. At the front was the showroom, and at the far end was the counter with the sheet music and gramophone records. To the left there was a long corridor with a curtain across.

In the shop, two rooms were built. One was for us to use, the other was sound-proofed for potential customers to listen to their records on an RGD radiogram or on an HMV one.

Through the curtain there were rooms for everything, with toilets at the end, by the back entrance. The first windowless room was the wireless room, with all makes of wirelesses on shelves round the walls. Other rooms were workshops for piano repairs and renovating old pianos. There was also a room for radio repairs, which was vast and often full of people. Then there was Mr Wise's office. There was quite a staff – a van driver, three piano tuners, repair boys and us girls. Kath was eighteen, Muriel was twenty-four, and I was twenty by then. Muriel and I were both new.

We were proud of our new shop. We had all helped to move the things from the old shop, which was now closed. The Stafford Road shop, however, was kept open.

Mr Wise had us measured for dresses. It was late autumn. He didn't allow heat in the showroom, because of the pianos, but we had an electric fire in our restroom. The dresses were of green wool, with velvet collars. I was so pleased, as my own clothes weren't warm enough for this large north-east-facing shop.

The pianos were displayed in rows, a Bechstein in front of the main row, with uprights on the narrow right-hand side. The Bechstein was £112, a Challen retailed at £90 and a Chappell cost £80. The cheapest were the second-hand renovated ones. Piano tuners often came into the shop to buy renovated ones. They were all nice friendly men.

My first job each day was to dust all the pianos, then sort out and tidy the music sheets, ready for the music teachers to choose and play. It was a riot of activity, with customers in and out all day, many paying instalments on their purchases.

In quiet times, we were allowed to play any piano. Muriel (Gilly we called her) was a born musician. She could play jazz, classics and all dance music by ear. Kath had a fair right hand, but her bass hand wandered anywhere! I could only read music, because of my strict teaching for the LRAM. My hands were covered up in my early lessons, with my eyes set firmly only on the music. We used to play all together if the shop was extra-quiet.

Mr Wise wore a black trilby and a long black overcoat, and he drove a Ford car. He had piercing blue eyes, was kind but very strict. Sometimes we would be talking – giggling about something – and the curtain would swish aside and he would say, "Get on with your work, please." Then he would go and make tea, bring it in, then go and get the whisky bottle and pour some into our cups. "That will warm you up," he would say. I never liked it, but tea always seemed flat without it.

Rob and I wrote to each other daily. He hadn't found a job, but spent his time with the maid, when he was indoors!

I was in the shop when disaster struck our family. Father was taken away to Brixton Prison for outstanding debt to the council. His job automatically ended. As he was 'in the law', he was instantly dismissed.

I asked Mr Wise why he hadn't warned me, or tried to appeal on behalf of my father. He said the debt was too great, and so it had to be.

I spent my twenty-first birthday with a tearful mother, and I gave my whole £1 wages to her – there was no money in the house. It was 1935.

Mr Wise gave us a big box of food for our Christmas, but his generosity was greeted with abuse, and my mother said she 'would hang before eating charity'. However, the food was used. The turkey was cooked by Mr Doick, the baker, and I carried it back home on Christmas Day – a 20lb bird on a large metal tray.

Whilst serving his time, Father wrote an article for the *News Chronicle* about Brixton Prison and soon after was back home without job or money.

Rob decided to return to Charles and Alice, much to their relief. Trade wasn't good without him, and they very nearly closed down. But all shops were suffering at that time.

It was depression also at home. One night in late January, I was in bed suffering from a bad dose of flu when a row started between

Betty and Mother. My father, in temper, lashed out and hit Betty several times and tore her thin clothes off her.

I sprung out of bed and quickly dressed. I grabbed two coats out of the wardrobe and took Betty up to our local police station in the Stafford Road. We were both in tears, and begged them to find somewhere for us to go.

A policeman went off to Sandy End, leaving us in their office. When he came back, he said, "The man was very ratty and his wife spiteful."

It was decided to send Betty to a rescue home, and they asked me if I had any friends I could go to. Betty was nineteen and I was twenty-one. I said my boss might help me, as he knew about my family troubles, and he would still be in his office. Mr Wise took me to his house in Redford Avenue, but Mrs Wise said they must not get involved.

So Mr Wise took me to Charles and Alice on this cold and frosty night at 9 p.m. They were both in bed. Rob was over at Kenton with his father, to answer an advert about a job in clothing. Charles stayed in bed, but Alice got up and told Mr Wise I could stay for the night and then see Mr Wise next day.

I remember their warm sitting room. Alice got me a hot-water bottle, then took me to the bathroom and gave me a large scented nightdress from the airing cupboard, and I went to bed in their little bedroom.

Next morning, there was a calm atmosphere and a lovely feeling of quietness. I got up to find that Alice had already gone off to Wallington. Charles came in later from Covent Garden Market. He smiled at me and said, "So you have left home at last, have you? Don't worry, you can stay here and see what can turn up for you and Rob."

They had a piano, and I played this until I needed some dinner. I went down to Manor Road, and told Mr Wise that I was going to stay with Charles and Alice. All my things were at Sandy End, so Mr Wise took me up to ask for them. Mother opened the door and refused to let me have anything – my home was there, she said!

Mr Wise saw Miss Lane, who kindly gave me underclothes, which she said were old but were good and thick, and I felt better and warmer.

We went next to Croydon to see Betty at a large house. The woman superintendent told me she had never had a more nervous girl of nineteen, unable to speak to her, and that she would stay there. She said the NSPCC would be told and would see me later, but I must be aware that Joyce could be taken away too!

I wrote to the NSPCC and said Joyce was not subjected to any cruelty, and neither was she shy or unhappy, but would be safe in Mother's care. However, she disliked Father completely. I hoped, therefore, she would be able to stay with Mother.

Then I wrote a long letter to Rob, and posted both of them off. Next morning, at the shop, at 9. 15 a.m., the phone rang for me. Rob asked what on earth was the letter in my handwriting about, and I realised I had put the letters in the wrong envelopes and had written in loving terms to the NSPCC man!

I thought the man would think I was mischief-making, but I need not have worried. He came to see me and assured me that Betty would be cared for specially by Miss Dowding. He said I must visit Betty regularly. I went over often, and Miss Dowding would tell me that she took Betty round in her car to show her the other world and try to get her to talk. Betty used to say, "I hate folk; they bother me."

Rob had now started a job as a salesman but, at Alice's invitation, came back to live with us all. Rob had the little room, I had the middle room, and my life was happy.

Neither Rob nor I were as close as sweethearts. We were more like friends, and one day Alice said, "You two have been going out for years – why don't you get married now?"

Rob's best friend, Stanley Cole, who was Charles's younger brother, got married to Eva in March 1936. They had a church ceremony, and Rob was best man. The wedding reception was held in Eva's parents' house in Fulham. I was a guest and among real happy cockneys – noisy loud people full of fun and laughter – beer and ale, and a piano. Eva's sister, Flo, thumped out 'My Old Man Said Foller the Van' and many many more.

On our way home we talked about our future. It wasn't promising, but at least we were both in work.

We decided that May would be when we got wed, but Rob flatly refused a church service. I said, "Just hat and coat, not white, but to have God's blessing."

Rob said, "If that is so important to you, we must part." He refused absolutely to have a church wedding.

CHAPTER FIVE

The 27th May was our wedding day at 3 p.m. at Epsom Register Office. I worked until 1 p.m. and Rob did the same, then we dressed for our wedding. Charles and Alice were our witnesses, and Charles drove us all there in his new car.

My coat was £1, my blue dress 10/-, a hat 5/-, shoes and gloves 10/-, and I felt good in the new clothes. Rob had a £2 suit with waistcoat and black shoes. We each wore a buttonhole – Rob had a carnation, whilst I had three pink orchids.

Gilly, from Wise's, had a sister who worked for Moyses Stevens, the royal florists, and she got them for us at cost price.

The 27th happened also to be Derby Day. George V had died in January, and Edward VIII was due to be crowned king. When we came out just married from the register office, people were already coming back down from the racecourse. "He's picked a winner," one man called out through the railings.

Mr Wise had no idea I was getting married, as he never employed married women. I planned to take off my ring every day and leave it at home.

I had booked two seats at the Adelphi Theatre to see *Follow the Sun*, through Keith Prowse at the shop, and everyone thought it was a grand night out.

The next day Mr Wise found out, and sent for me. He said he would allow me to stay without a ring and remain Miss Wontner, so all was well.

All that summer, on a Sunday, we got up at 6 a.m. and cycled across London to Sunbury-on-Thames. Since boyhood Rob had loved fishing, and he bought us both a rod and all the fishing gear. I was used to early mornings, and I enjoyed cycling through very quiet London roads.

We would settle down on the riverbank opposite holiday shacks. They had names like Drop In and Weir In, and each had a garden front and a boat tied up. The river smell and lovely fresh air was all new to me.

Nearby, my father-in-law had a large place. It was an old wartime circular corrugated shed on stilts, with built-on wooden rooms. It was right next to the Weir Hotel, and was in its grounds. He called it Otazel, and I learned long after that it was Hot-as-Hell. Marjory knew nothing about it, and father-in-law would bring his friends there and enjoy the Weir Hotel ambience and amicable company.

He told us we could have it for a week in August for a belated honeymoon. That week, every day, Rob fished, standing in the fast-flowing weir opposite. I would row food over to him, and once I nearly rowed into and over the weir! My honeymoon consisted of just sitting, knitting, cooking and cleaning up the shack.

Rob caught a very large fish – a roach. He put it on a large dish and I photographed him with his prize. Then he told me to soak it in salt water, to cook the next day. It tasted awful! At the end of that week, we returned to Wallington, and went back to work.

Rob had liked his job at Kenton as a salesman, so he got in touch with one of the men there and got a job again. This meant I had to leave my home and familiar surroundings, and give in my notice to Mr Wise. He was cross and said he had wasted time on training me, and it was a pity I had married as I was giving up a good future.

One Saturday, we left Wallington to go and live at Neasden, in a room over a shop on the main read. Next morning I went out to get food, as Rob told me Jews' shops were open on Sundays. The traffic was fast, noisy and the smells nasty, and I felt very unhappy but thought Rob knew where our future lay, so I must go along with it. It was all very strange to me, after my rural upbringing. Rob, however, had been brought up in London and was very much at home and very optimistic.

We both had bikes to get around on, and I had had a happy summer. We had punt outings on the Thames, six of us, with one bringing a portable wind-up gramophone to enjoy the music under the sun-shading overhanging trees.

I had done a lot of gardening for Charles. He had laid out his garden in grass terraces. I cut these, did the edges and weeded. At the bottom of the garden, Charles grew a row of runner beans, which were poor and only had small beans hanging on them. We used to bring our bikes into the back, through the gate. One night, I saw a long green bean hanging. I went to Charles to tell him, and as he came out to see, I saw Rob's grinning face, and we found he had brought the bean from out of the shop and wired it on.

I missed all this greatly at Neasden. I didn't like it at all, but Rob was happy and enthusiastic. In October, we moved nearby, into two rooms, and we ordered some furniture on hire purchase.

By now, I was working at Woolworth's, without ring, and I was called Miss Riches. Nothing on the papers I handed to the manager showed I was married. I was put on the gramophone-and-fancy-goods counter, on my own by the door. I played Vera Lynn singing 'When the Poppies Bloom Again' very often. It was then the top popular record.

I learned that Mother and Father had been turned out of Sandy End due to large debts, and they were now lodging at their doctor's house.

Betty was working as a cinema usherette and still living with Miss Dowding at the rescue home. She wrote to us telling us about the home, and how she had a liking for her cinema life in the dark.

I would leave for work at 8.45 a.m., leaving Rob, who cycled to his job. We both had our Thursday afternoons off and usually went to the pictures. Walking back home, we would stop and buy a small cake for 4½d, for a treat.

Rob worked for a man called Digby, who ran a clothing club from his own house and paid Rob £2 a week. He cycled his rounds in North-West London, wearing a trilby hat and raincoat. My wage was £1 per week.

We paid 13/- a week for our rooms; rent of a gas cooker was 1/-; we paid a further 1/- for gas; and 1/- for the electric light. I also managed to save 1/- a week since we got married.

To stock up with necessities for our home, I had a 10/- voucher to use at Woolworth's. All items were 3d or 6d, and every week there was a 1d counter for chipped or dirty goods. We now had four place settings in china and cutlery, as well as a few 1d chipped-glass dishes and basins. All our other needs came from that 10/- voucher. We had to take a basket on a trolley and fill it with penny items. I enjoyed doing that and was proud of our emerging new home.

In November, I came home one Friday night to find Rob already home, looking very glum. On Fridays he would normally be out until 10 or 11 p.m., as it was the best collecting evening of the week. "Digby has gone broke, so he's sacked me," he said.

1936, still in the depression, had few jobs except labouring, such as road-sweeping, for very poor wages. I said, "With my £1 and your 15/- dole money, we could still manage."

With Christmas ahead, we had an unexpected letter from my father. He wrote that he, Mother and Joyce now lodged with one of his legal friends, and had got a job in Redhill as a solicitor's managing clerk.

The friend, who was elderly, lived in Ewell, and he and his wife offered Christmas invitations to Rob and me, as well as Betty. Rob said no, and meant it. I thought about the prospect of spending Christmas in just two rooms with very little money, so I begged him to say yes and he reluctantly agreed. The Underground and Southern Railway journey to Ewell would cost very little, and we could walk to their house from the station.

Rob managed to get a Christmas job at W. H. Smith's bookshop and worked until 10 p.m. He came home at 11 p.m. on Christmas Eve, and next morning woke with a headache. On the tube he was very unwell.

At Ewell, with just 10/- in our pockets, I called a taxi and we arrived at the friends' home with Rob really poorly. They were very kind, and took Rob up to the single bedroom, which both of us were to share, whilst I joined my family in their lounge.

The elderly man was a diabetic; the woman was plump and jolly. "Dinner is cooking," the woman told me. She would have chicken, but my father had bought a turkey for all of us. Chicken in 1936 was a real luxury.

As Rob was lying down, I was told to ask him what he would like to eat. He replied, "Nothing, thank you," so I went downstairs and we ate our Christmas dinner without him.

In the afternoon, I saw some watercress in a basin and, knowing it was a favourite of Rob's, asked if I could put some in a sandwich, to tempt him. Mother said it would be all right, and Rob sat up and ate it all, to my great relief.

Later, the man asked who had taken some of his tea. It was all part of his diet and he needed it all. They were very nice about it, so I didn't feel too guilty. Christmas Day was kept very quiet, but Boxing Day was full of fun and games.

Rob and I returned to Neasden and back to work, just for me. Woolworth's had their yearly stocktaking so, although closed, we were all busy counting and cleaning our individual counters.

Early in 1937, souvenirs were being sold off cheaply for the cancelled coronation of Edward VIII, and some were on my counter at 3d and 6d each. With George VI souvenirs due, these soon sold, and I foolishly never thought to buy a single one of them.

In March I became pregnant again. The first time, soon after we married, was speedily ended by Rob giving me hot gin and a soap-and-water douche. I accepted the situation then. We had been living in Charles and Alice's home, and had no future to plan for.

This was the second time. Rob was now working again and we were renting two comfortable rooms, but Rob said, "If you wanted a family, you have married the wrong chap." We had never talked about having children, but my ambition was a happy home with children, so I was shocked, but I let Rob administer his 'cure'!

Nothing happened, so I bought some wool and when Rob came home he found me knitting. He said, "So, you have made up your mind to have the kid, have you?" I said I had, and life went on as usual.

At Woolworth's, I now found I couldn't stand for hours, so I gave in my notice to my boss, Mr Smith. He was a nice man and despite my protesting I couldn't do figure work, he put me up in the office and bought me a ready reckoner to help me.

I hated it so much that after a fortnight I told him I must leave. He said, so as I would get dole money straight away, he would say he sacked me as I couldn't do clerical work.

Next day I walked from Neasden to Hendon, all along the North Circular Road to Staples Corner, then turning left to Hendon. Outside the labour exchange I found a queue of noisy women waiting, and I joined them.

Inside, a man questioned me and asked if I intended to find another job. I said I had no experience other than shop work. He said I must attend a panel to decide if money was to be paid for six months, and this I did.

I sat facing a row of men, and was asked if I intended to work after my baby was born. I wasn't sure about my answer – I certainly didn't intend to work – but I'm glad I didn't say no. They said that unless I was going to return to work afterwards, I would not be entitled to more than six weeks' money. They conferred, then decided I would get six months' money till December.

I had to sign on three times a week. It was summer and the nice long walk was something I enjoyed.

But my days had a worry – had my baby been harmed by Rob's efforts to destroy it? – and I wondered, when the time was due, how it would come out of me. I had heard of childbirth pain, and I looked at girls pushing prams, all seemingly well and happy – so I thought, whatever happened, I would, come what may, soon be a mother.

Rob became hard and often strict. In front of people, he ridiculed some of my remarks and made me feel very low in self-esteem.

I sat often in the very overrun garden of our two rooms, and knitted. I used a fine two-ply wool, knitting vests, matinee coats and a shawl in a delicate pattern, and dreamed. I ate just a little at midday, then cooked the meat and two veg at night.

Washing-up was done in a bowl on the table. We had the use of the bathroom only once a week. The lavatory was separate. I washed our small things in the washbasin, and the large went into the 'bag wash' for 1/-. It always came back wrinkled and grey, but we kept clean.

I went to the clinic at Willesden in June. There, a big nurse with a harsh voice asked my age. I said twenty-three. She said, "Well, you look like a schoolgirl and far too young to have babies."

I visited Dr Jack in Tanfield Avenue every month, and I was to have my baby in Honeypot Lane at Kingsbury, a Willesden hospital.

Rob was now being employed by Bon Marche in Willesden, and earned about £2 10s, whilst I had my 15/- a week dole money. We then looked for a ground-floor flat with three rooms, and found a nice one in Kingsbury for £1 a week. It was owned by a man who cycled over every Sunday to collect his two rents, one up and one down.

When we looked over it, we found the back room had a French window with an open but covered verandah. The garden was divided into two, with a central concrete path separating them. On one side, I could see a baby kicking and gurgling in an open pram. It was September.

A very fat young woman appeared through the side gate and said she was Mrs Lawrence, and the baby was Beryl. She lived upstairs, and her husband worked quite nearby and was home every evening at six o'clock.

I wondered why she hadn't taken the downstairs flat. Their side of the garden was on the left-hand side, with a shed at the bottom. Later, we found that Mr Lawrence spent more time in his shed than in his home, and every Sunday morning he was always in it. They were an odd couple; he was thin, and she was fat.

Rob said the garden we had would be split into two halves. I could grow the flowers, and he would grow the vegetables. The grass lawn was small and bordered the path.

Our furniture in the two rooms at Neasden had been just a dining-room suite with a lovely oak-veneered sideboard and a tapestry bed-settee with two fireside chairs.

For our Kingsbury flat, we bought a second-hand bedroom suite, a wardrobe with a mirror door and drawer, and a two-drawer chest. My parents later sent a cot, substantially made with wide bars, bucket ends and a horsehair mattress. An enclosed letter said cots were dangerous usually.

This was a complete surprise, but we were very grateful as no interest in us had been shown before or asked for.

Rob's father had visited us briefly at Neasden, and Marjory, bless her, came to help with our move. I had given up on my parents – they were sufficient unto themselves.

Through that autumn we lived comfortably. My baby was expected on 7th December.

I went to Dr Jack regularly. He was enthusiastic about me and said, "You are healthy and young – the best thing."

I went afterwards to Rob's friend's sister, Ada, who had just moved to Neasden from Fulham, and I had tea with her. I told her that I hoped I wouldn't have pains on a Friday, as it was Rob's late night, with him sometimes not coming home until 11 p.m. after a long cycle ride from London.

I loved Kingsbury. It was not busy, and had green spaces with shops at the top of our road – Meadowbank Road. There was a paper shop, a nice grocer and a curtain-and-cushion shop.

The grocer sold Wiltshire roll bacon, and sold little bits to use for dripping etc. The paper-shop man was related to Spencer, the artist. Both he and his sister were friendly and chatty.

On 26th November I went to see Dr Jack as usual. It was very cold and foggy, and I was wearing a thin dress, with the coat I got married in, and a thin rubber macintosh over the top of it. I was very large, but always felt the cold. Dr Jack said all was well and hoped I had better weather for my confinement.

I then went round, as usual, to Ada and had a chatty tea with her. She said I must get the bus back early, as the fog was so thick.

Suddenly a pain shook me. I said I had had some steak for dinner and it must be indigestion. I left and took the bus, getting off at the top of my road. A bad pain hit me once again, and I had to cling to the pillar box until the pain went.

Indoors, I had sheets and washing hanging in the kitchen. It was 9 p.m. so I went straight to bed. More pain made me call out, and Mrs Lawrence came down. Looking grim, she said, "Yes, you are for it – I hope your husband comes soon."

Thankfully, Rob came home at 10 p.m. He immediately went out to the nearby phone box and phoned for a taxi. The fog was so awful that the taxi man got a policeman to sit in the open front, and we crawled to Honeypot Lane. I was now in regular agony. As we got to the hospital, I heard a baby crying and thought, 'At last I am giving birth!'

Inside, I was plunged into a warm bath, then put into a little room and left alone. I went through hell. I was terrified and very upset. A nurse came in and sternly said, "Be quiet! Mothers are trying to sleep in here," and went back out.

I continued to shriek and moan through the night, when suddenly a plate was put beside me and I was told to eat my breakfast. Then I was whipped out of bed and put on a table with a pillow, and my baby came at 8.30 a.m. All was peaceful, then I heard a cry and asked, "What is it, please?"

"You have a son. We shall take him away for now; you will see him later."

I was thrilled – an eldest son for my family. I would be forty-four when he was twenty-one. I was full of joy and love for my baby.

Then I was wheeled into a large ward with beds on either side and told I would be in bed for a fortnight; and, exhausted, I fell asleep.

Upon waking up, I saw opposite me a woman with an Eton crop and a white face. She asked me what I had had, a boy or girl?

"A boy," I answered.

"I wanted a boy," she lamented. "I didn't want a girl."

She told me she was forty, and this was her first baby. It was lucky to be born, she was told.

At about four o'clock in the afternoon, a bundle was put into my arms. I asked if he was all right, and I was told yes. I looked at the tiny wizened face, his eyes shut tight, and I kissed him. Then I began to look at his hands – they were perfect, with white, oval nails. I carefully took off the bootees, and saw that, on his right foot, two toes were joined together. I had been looking for defects because of my awful secret.

I began to cry, and the nurse asked what was wrong. I told her, "He isn't perfect."

She laughed and said, "He's lovely. What name shall I put on his wrist?"

If a girl, Rob and I had settled for Grace – his mother's name; if a boy, either Michael or Brian. I liked Michael, but told the nurse I must ask my husband.

"I must put something –" she said, adding, "you can change it." I said, "Michael."

In the evening Rob arrived, having cycled through thick snow. He was carrying a faded bunch of maroon chrysanthemums.

He was taken to the nursery to see his baby, and upon returning said, "I see he is Michael."

I said it wasn't his name – it could be changed to Brian.

Rob said, "It is on his wrist – he is Michael."

He didn't stay, saying he would come back tomorrow with his father and Marjory.

The next day, Sunday afternoon, they arrived. Marjory sat down and said, "It's another boy – that's all the Riches family can produce," and she put a quick-knit beige pram cover on the bed.

Rob's father said little, and looked bored.

Suddenly Ada and her friend appeared, clutching flowers and a carrier bag. She called out loudly, "There she is," and trotted up to my bed.

Only two visitors were allowed, and father-in-law didn't need moving by force. He jumped up and said he and Marjory must go.

Ada had a cleft palette, and spoke loudly, but she was kind-hearted and well meaning and had brought magazines and sweets with her. She also gave me a hand-knitted coat for Michael, which was very grubby. She said her hands got bad in winter, but it was all new wool.

After a fortnight, I was told to get up. I could hardly stand, I was so weak. It was bitterly cold, and Christmas Day was only two weeks away.

Rob, now working in the clothing trade, bought me a coat for £1, bottle-green worsted, which was very warm and very smart.

I knitted Michael another pair of white bootees, to hang on his cot for his present.

On Christmas Eve, Rob came home with a chicken, hanging fully feathered on his bike's handlebars: "For you to see to," he said! Snow was lying thickly and it was very cold, but we had a good fire, with a back boiler for hot water. I decided to bath Mike at night, wrap him up and then put him to bed. The bedroom was unheated and the cot large for a 6½lb baby. I went in and out of the room often to make sure he was breathing all right.

Our bed had our coats on top of the two blankets covering us, but we managed to get by fairly well.

For the first three months, Michael cried, and I walked him about on my hip as I did my housework. When Rob worked late, I took Michael out, with a pot of honey in the bottom of the pram, and a dummy in his mouth. He was very aware of everything, and gazed at all that went near his vision.

January and February 1938 were dull with snow and ice. Nothing dried out of doors. I had only two changes of clothing and twelve towelling nappies, which I aired and dried in front of the fire, but I managed to keep Mike clean.

March came in like a dream, with sunshine every day. It was a truly lovely month and Kingsbury and the outskirts started to look green and pretty once again.

1938 was a happy year. I loved my little home, all cleaned and polished. I walked to Kingsbury village with my friend Winnie, just married and living with some relatives nearby. I had worked with Winnie at Woolworth's and now she too was married – to Stan Broadbridge, who drove a laundry van – and we all got together in the evenings.

Winnie and Stan weren't happy living with their relatives, and one night we suggested that we rent a house and share it.

Rob had heard that the house opposite our previous two rooms at Neasden was to be let. It was better for Rob cycling home, and Stan and Winnie's parents' homes were nearby. It had a large garden which was south-facing, and the kitchen and sitting room overlooked it.

The owner owned a lot of houses, and employed an agent who lived close by. The agent told us the house would be redecorated, and we could choose the wallpapers.

We decided it would be a good move for all of us. The Neasden shops were good, and just half a mile away along the North Circular Road. There was a new library near us, and the recreation ground looked over the Welsh Harp at Hendon. I felt better about living at

Mother at Mellows Road, 1920.

Gladys and Betty at Mellows Road, 1920.

Uncle Vic (Nunkie) at Mellows Road, 1920.

Aunty Mary and Benny with Grandpa's cherry tree behind.

Grandpa and Grandma Wontner in their garden at Mitcham.

Gladys with Joyce, 9 months old, at Mellows Road, 1922.

Betty, Margie, Gladys and Joyce, 1924.

Betty, Joyce and Gladys with Father behind.

Betty, Joyce and Gladys at Shoreham, 1927.

Gladys and Eileen Wise at Shoreham 1931.

Gladys on Ranmore Common, 1932.

Gladys and Rob on their wedding day, outside Epsom Register Office, 27th May 1936.

Charlie Cole, Alice Cole, Gladys and Rob, 27th May 1936.

Rob fishing on honeymoon at Sunbury Weir, August 1936.

Gladys on honeymoon at Sunbury Weir, August 1936.

Gladys with Michael in Gladstone Park, 1938.

Michael and Gladys at Sunbury-on-Thames, 1943.

Marjory, Grandpa Riches, Michael and Gladys, 1939.

Rob on duty at Staverton Airfield, 1941.

Rob with Michael at Churchdown, 1942.

Ray Pope, 1942.

Rob and Michael fishing at Wainlode Hill, 1943.

Rob, Michael and Gladys, Neasden, 1938.

Gladys, Evelyn and Michael at Bristol, September 1945.

Rob and Gladys back together, at Kings Langley, June 1946.

Gladys, Michael and Rob at Holidays, Shoreham, 1949.

60 Ferrymead Gardens, Greenford, nearing completion, September 1950.

Rob with Michael, Kingsbury, 1938.

Neasden, because it was better for Rob, Win and Stan. Win's mother could visit her more easily; and she liked me, saying I was a sensible friend.

Winnie fell pregnant, and had a little girl. They named her Yvonne. I used to think how lovely it would be if Mike and Yvonne married one day.

The house was very homely, with the kitchen having a larder cupboard with two doors, one from the kitchen and one into the sitting room, so I could keep an eye on Mike playing in the warm room. We kept a shelf empty so we could pass our meals through, which was very handy.

The house opposite us was called Guimaral. It was owned by a good-looking Italian man and his wife, whose surname was Lorro. They lived next door to our old two rooms, and I used to hear Mr Lorro (Alberto) sing a lot. I got to know them well. They had three sons: Guido, seventeen; Mario, fifteen; and Albert, thirteen. Mrs Lorro told me she had agreed to her husband choosing the names of Guido and Mario, but had her wish by calling the last baby Albert. I liked the house name, and thought it very clever.

Mr Lorro was the head waiter at the London Casino, and gave many famous stage and film stars his personal service. I remember the star who sang 'Pennies from Heaven' giving Mr Lorro a copy of it, to take home to his wife. He used to tell me all about his work life, and he loved it.

Winnie and I tackled a big lawn full of plantain. After dinner, we got on our knees and dug out piles of it. Our neighbours from Kingsbury gave us an old mower, and I mowed and tugged it over the grass every week. These ex-neighbours also gave us some plants with which to stock the garden.

They gave us helenium in autumn colours, goldenrod, and dull brown chrysanthemums, which bloomed in November and made the beds look very nice.

Michael, now eighteen months old, loved his playground, and he lived out there during the summer days.

One day, he started to cry on and off. Winnie's mother, Mrs Spencer, told me he was cutting his wisdom teeth, and suggested I should go and buy Steedman's teething powder, and put it in some milk before going to bed. I read the words on the packet, and only gave him half the dose.

About 4.30 a.m. he woke and asked for 'putty'. He passed number twos rapidly, and, within a short time, again. This continued and then I saw blood. Then Michael went limp; he had fallen asleep, we thought. Rob went up to Dr Jack, just along the road. I kept a sample for him.

He looked at it and said, "Lumme! he must go to hospital."

I said, "I could look after him."

Dr Jack said, "He is very ill."

Soon after, an ambulance arrived. It was 6 a.m. and I had dressed earlier. I had a long apron on, and Rob was in shirt and trousers. The ambulance man said, "You can come," so we just jumped in. It was May and it was a beautiful morning.

At the hospital, Michael was whisked away. Matron saw us in her office, and told us, "Michael is so ill, and we might lose him." She continued: "I expect he is christened."

I said, "No."

She asked, "Why?"

I replied, "We hadn't got round to it." I couldn't tell her that Rob had refused 'such a stupid thing'.

Matron said, "I suppose you won't object to me administering it, if it is necessary?"

I said, "No, of course not."

We were told to leave and visit in the afternoon. We were miles from home, it was a Sunday, and I felt awful in my old dress and carrying my pinny.

Rob said, "Why is christening so special and needed?"

I told him, "Michael would not lie in consecrated ground if he died."

"Well, if he lives, you had better fix it up," he said in a cross way.

Michael had intussusception of his bowel, and he was immediately operated on.

Dr Jack had seen the packet of Steedman's on the bedroom shelf, and had said, "You mothers will take such things. Only give a child liquid paraffin or milk of magnesia in future."

Michael lived. He was kept in hospital for a week, and, when I went to bring him home, I took his little pushchair.

Back at home, he sat on the settee straight-faced, and wet it! He had been clean for almost six months, so I had to start all over again.

I took him to the Church of England vicar's house and arranged a christening date for 2nd July, at St Catherine's, Neasden.

Winnie and Stan's baby daughter, Yvonne, was not yet christened, and Winnie said, "Let's make it a double. We'll have it at Mum's."

I was so pleased and grateful.

I knitted myself a short-sleeved jumper to go with my one skirt, and Mike wore rompers made by Joe's wife, Gladys, in silky yarn, and I felt very proud.

Winnie's mother baked a cake and laid a nice tea. The day was warm and sunny.

Rob had his half-day on a Thursday, and would eat his dinner and then sleep all the afternoon, and exactly the same on Sundays. We never went out together, and he refused to see to Mike, or push his pram.

I said I would love to go for a walk one afternoon. Rob said, "Where? Up one road and down the other? No thanks! Go by yourself if you want to." I was so upset inside. Rob was always strict in his ways with me. He criticised my work: cupboards were untidy and I was lazy. He pulled the contents of the stair cupboard out all over the floor.

One day, a man called at the door, offering an enlargement of a photo free; so I gave him the last one that was taken of Michael – a nice studio coloured one. He got me to sign for a frame, at 1/- a week. It was very nice. I thought Rob would be very pleased.

When I told him he shouted at me: "You must not buy at the door." He snatched the receipt of 1/- off me, went to a call box and demanded the return of the photo.

I was so hurt and very upset over it. I couldn't think that I had done wrong. It took a long time before the roughened photo was returned.

It started a pattern of harsh opinions of any of my doings. I spoke to a lady I knew about it, and she said, "I never let my husband know all I do. All men are selfish!"

From time to time, if we argued, Rob would say, "Just like your mother," and I was hurt. My opinions had been squashed by Mother all my life, and I now found myself in the same situation; and I was not allowed the freedom Winnie and Stan shared.

Rob wanted his own way and displayed fierce outbursts of temper. When he came home at night, he turned on the wireless, ate his dinner in silence, and had little to say. If he did say something, it would be about one of his customers. I was never asked about Michael or myself.

CHAPTER SIX

There were worrying radio announcements about Germany and Hitler, and the threat of possible outbreak of war. Older people took it seriously, but it didn't worry me.

Things had improved so much in Britain: there was more employment (the Midlands especially drew many people to work in the growing car industry); and more goods appeared in the shops. In 1938 our life was less frugal. Wages were better for Rob, as more people bought clothes and furnishings, by paying weekly 1/- in the pound.

Rob's hours became longer, and he used to eat out more frequently. Michael and I hardly saw him, and my life was becoming more and more lonely. I would see other husbands at home with their families, and it was making me very envious, but Rob was so keen – selling was in his blood. He said many times that he liked being free, without anyone telling him what to do.

One night he came home upset. His takings had been lost – stolen, he thought. The firm's ruling was strict: each man was responsible for all his money.

I said, "We must pay it off somehow."

Rob said he expected me to be cross.

I said, "It was an accident, and it has to be faced." The sum, lost or stolen, was £10.

We borrowed £5 from Rob's father, and Mr Lee, Rob's boss said he would take Rob's week's holiday away that year, for the other £5.

Rob's father was paid back regularly. We never questioned how a father, so well off, could see a son struggle to pay it.

In 1938 £5 bought a lot. Whole dining suites were £10, and a suit at Burton's would cost £2 10s. Not a lot of people today would understand that. The quality and workmanship of such items were excellent. They were of good value and built to last. Our oak-veneered and part-solid dining suite was £19 19s, and I still have the sideboard to this day. We collected our home in stages, and I was very proud of it all.

My housekeeping money was £1 10s weekly. Our weekly bill for coal (1 cwt) was 2/6d, gas was 1/-, electric 1/-, and we saved 1/- in our post office savings account.

My grocery cost 10/- a week, ordered at Williams Stores, and delivered. The weekend joint was 2/6d, and, for the rest of the week, it was liver, hearts, or pieces of beef or veal for casseroles, and the gravies you got from them. Then we would have fish on Fridays and sausages on Saturdays. Greengrocery and fruit were bought daily.

I baked cakes and made pastry every week, so we ate well. The gas cooker and the copper were both of grey enamel, and easy to clean.

Joe, Gladys and Phil came for Christmas Day 1938, and Joe brought a large leg of pork. He was full of praise, because I cooked it well. Sage grew in our garden, and I used it to make the stuffing. I had made the pudding and mince pies, so we all ate in style. It was nice to leave behind our first Christmas and the struggles we had endured.

Soon war was looming, and, by August 1939, warnings about bombs and gas were worrying. We were advised to seal all windows by sticking paper strips over the gaps, and to have black curtains.

The week before war was declared, Joe came to tell us that he had joined the Irish Rifles, and left home. Gladys came round soon after, worried over their dog, Major, an Alsatian, who was pining for Joe and wouldn't eat.

A few days later, Joe suddenly turned up to tell me he was being sent abroad, and had a day off. He didn't want to go home and asked me not to tell Gladys. I decided to cook tripe for him and Rob, as they both loved it. I told Joe I would go down to the butcher's – Michael was in bed. It was 7.30 p.m. and Rob was due in at nine o'clock. So I set out. Everywhere was pitch black, with no lights on the North Circular Road. I was very scared, and I rushed to the butcher's, bought the tripe and ran back home. I never went out in the dark for ages afterwards. Joe slept on our put-you-up, and left next morning. He looked very smart in his uniform with the green flash in his cap.

On 3rd September we received a great blow – the speech and declaration of war, and then immediately the siren sounded.

Stan came downstairs and said he would take Winnie and the baby in his van to relations in Surrey, before coming back here to continue doing his job.

My parents were, as usual, on their annual holiday in Shoreham, at Mrs Wise's railway-carriage bungalow (two carriages with verandahs all round).

Rob cycled to Joe's house and took his modern Land Rover. We packed cot, pushchair and clothes inside, and drove down to Sussex. It was a lovely day, and the roads were empty. I remember seeing a man with a gas mask on his back, picking blackberries in a Sussex lane.

When we arrived at Kings Drive, on Shoreham front, we found Mother, Father and Joyce sitting in the sun, on the pebbled beach. My sister Betty and her boyfriend were there also, sitting on the verandah of the bungalow.

To my relief, there was a spare bed for me, so Rob left and I settled to this new unexpected move.

A week later, Rob arrived back in the Land Rover. Nothing had happened in the week; the siren had been a false alarm and Winnie had returned, so we went back home to Neasden.

Winnie's mother came round and mournfully said, "Life is going to be awful for us all." We didn't know what she knew and could foresee. It depressed us both, but life went on as before.

Michael was two years old in November, and we had a party for him. Winnie's Yvonne was still a baby; we had her and other toddlers for a muted celebration. A month later it was Christmas, and we spent this quietly.

After Christmas it turned very cold. It snowed and was so icy that our back boiler froze, so there was no hot water or fire!

I lit a fire in the bedroom grate, and lived in there for quite a while. Mike played happily with his box of toys and books, and I knitted a pale-mauve jumper for myself – the wool cost 3¾d an ounce. All Michael's clothes were made from two-ply (his vests) and three-ply (his jumper suits and socks).

In June 1940, Rob came home very pleased – he and Stan Cole, had gone to the RAF to join up. "We don't want the bloody infantry," Rob said.

I asked, "How long will it be before you go?"

Rob replied, "Soon, I hope."

Notice was quickly given that on 2nd July he had to go up to Blackpool to report.

That morning I cooked him bacon, egg, kidneys, tomatoes and fat bread for his breakfast. He kissed me and he was gone.

I was alone and frightened, I had 29/- a week income, and the future is another story – a long one.

CHAPTER SEVEN

When the front door closed after Rob had gone off to join the RAF, I had a lot to face alone and a lot to decide about Michael's and my future. Now I was responsible for the 32/- rent of the house. Winnie and Stan paid 14/- for the upstairs, whilst we paid the balance of 18/-. My RAF money would now be only 29/- a week, so I knew I must tell the agent I had to leave.

I told Win and Stan that I had to give up the tenancy. Stan was now working as a progress chaser in war work and earned a better wage. Winnie said they would look right away for a flat near her mother. I was relieved that I hadn't upset them, as they had made it into a very comfortable home.

Gladys came round as usual, and when I told her Rob had gone and about my problem, she said, "Go home to your mother and dad."

I had previously taken Joe in his uniform and Gladys to Wallington to see the house my parents had taken on a weekly rent. It had been left empty due to the war, and was large, detached, and had a long overgrown garden. Mother seemed much better and we enjoyed a nice day and took photos.

I wanted to feel safe, so it seemed the right thing to do, and my money would be best spent there.

Gladys said she would take my main furniture for me and put it among hers, with the bedroom furniture being stored in her empty back room.

Gladys had a good job in London as a machinist, making army clothing. My copper went into her kitchen, the cooker I left behind, whilst my various household goods I gave away to my near neighbours.

Rob's employer, Mr Lee, had told him I could get help from one

100

of his staff to take me anywhere I wanted. George Turner, who was forty and Rob's friend, took me, cot, pushchair and all my things over to Wallington. He sat in Mother's kitchen. Mother was in a strict mood and told me to go upstairs and put my things in the second bedroom with twin beds.

George left and our life changed completely. I knew straight away that I had made the wrong decision, as from then on Mother issued instructions about Michael, saying I was to go out to do the shopping and she would see to him.

Michael, missing his daddy and not happy to be at Briar End, cried a lot and refused food. Every afternoon, Mother would take him into the drawing room and lock the door, telling me, before she did this, that he needed to be talked to and taught good manners. I was so upset and afraid of her that I asked my father what I could do and how Mother had been in the years since I left home. He took me into his writing den. Mother was busy bathing Michael and she was singing loudly to him.

Dad told me she had caused trouble at his firm by phoning up constantly. In the end he had had to tell her that he didn't care how much of his money she spent or what she did with herself while he was at work, but he absolutely forbade any further phone calls to him and she had now stopped. He told me to be patient, as she obviously thought I was too young to teach Michael proper manners. He said Mother was envious that I had a son. With Mother now rowing over all I did, I was really fearful I would not have some sort of life with Michael.

One morning, soon after, when Mother was in her greenhouse, I rang Mr Lee and asked his advice. He said he would come immediately to get me, and, in the meantime, decide where I wanted to go. He said that George had told him that he hadn't been happy leaving me, as he could see that Mother was mental – he could see it in her face. I was very surprised, but so pleased and felt brave.

I went out in the garden and told Mother I was leaving and wanted all of Michael's clothes, which she had put away in the drawers. She was furious and said I could go to hell, but she would keep Michael there.

I packed up the cot, and put it outside with the pushchair. Mr Lee arrived soon after eleven o'clock in his firm's van.

Mother suddenly appeared, shouting, "Take Michael and get out!"

I asked for all the things I had brought. She threw them all out onto the driveway. Mr Lee picked them up and told me to go and sit in the van with Michael.

Mother shouted to Mr Lee, "That is all the thanks I get for being a good mother. Gladys is a bad girl."

We drove away. I was in tears of relief and so thankful Mr Lee had come. He was a very imposing man. Rob always called him sir and very much respected him. Mr Lee suggested that as my furniture was at my sister-in-law's, perhaps I could go there. I told him she was at work in London, so he said he would take me home. We stopped for a meal at one o'clock and arrived in Wembley where his house was at about two o'clock.

Mrs Lee was cross with him as she had had his dinner keeping hot in the oven, but she was nice to me. Michael played with their son, Robin, who was a month older than him. They also had a son aged eleven, and Mrs Lee was now in her thirties. About an hour after arriving, Mrs Lee said she and Mr Lee had talked, and would I like to live there and be her help in the house and cook sometimes? I was so pleased at their kind offer as I could also keep my 29/- RAF allowance. I was given a very nice bedroom, and their home was lovely to work in, with a big kitchen that had a water softener in it.

The next day, I got up early and put the cleaner and duster to work, then saw to Mike. We all breakfasted together.

Once a week a woman came to do cleaning as this was a large house with windows all round and two main outside doors.

I took the boys out into the park in the afternoons and I wrote a letter to Rob, who was still at Blackpool. He was so pleased to learn where I was and replied in his letter that he wondered if he had given my life alone any thought. I still felt that he had been thoughtless and selfish to go so quickly as the call-up had still not reached his age group.

I bought new clothes for both of us. Mr Lee then said I must come to work at their shop, just new and called 'Peter-Robins' (named after their two sons), and serve Friday afternoons and all day Saturdays. Mrs Lee would see to Mike, bath and put him to bed.

The shop was in Harlesden, opposite a large cinema, which had a Ginger Rogers film advertised. I took the bus from Wembley for sixpence, and enjoyed the shop work. But it didn't last. Michael cried non-stop and he was a job to feed and became constipated. So I went back to being nursemaid. Poor Michael was lost and unhappy away from his happy life at Neasden, but he was soon better and happy with me.

After only a month, Hitler bombed London. The Lees had an air-raid shelter built in the garden, which was well furnished for all six of us, and we went into this. I stayed upstairs with Michael, not very afraid as Wembley was 'suburbs' to me. However, Mr Lee said it was obvious the war was 'hotting up' and he thought it best for me to be with relatives. I reluctantly agreed. Times were worrying, and rationing was well and truly in now.

Gladys was happy to give us a home, so we moved in and I was in my own bed once again. Phil, Gladys's younger brother, now twenty-five, had the smaller front bedroom set up with a modern cabinet bed, which, when folded, looked like a polished flat cupboard. He worked in the local Co-op shop and had a half-day on Wednesday. Gladys hated cooking, and, to my surprise, ate from tins heated up. I used to buy minced beef for a pie with pastry top and bottom, and with onion and sliced potato in it. For me it was a usual midweek dish, and I offered it to Phil to share. He ate it up with relish and enthusiasm and he was full of praise. I knew now how poor his meals must be, and why Joe came to us on his days home. He too was always full of praise for my 'poor man's' simple meals, especially steamed fish with parsley sauce and mashed potatoes.

Phil was a warden, and soon bombs fell nearby, so each night we took our deckchairs to the street shelter, staying there till the all-clear siren sounded, usually about 4 a.m. I had Michael asleep in my arms all the time. It was now September and very chilly.

One day I was pushing Michael in his pushchair back from the Neasden shops to Kingsbury, when I saw planes overhead wheeling in and out in a clear blue sky. Then the siren sounded, and I ran with Michael to a large public shelter.

Gladys and Phil both said I ought to phone Rob's uncle and aunt at Uxbridge, where they rented a large farmhouse on Frays Farm. It was still being run as a dairy farm, and the cows were milked daily by farmhands.

Uncle Dick said I could come, so after only three weeks at Kingsbury he met us at Uxbridge Underground Station at 2 p.m. on a Saturday afternoon. It was a lovely sunny September day, and I remember standing waiting, with a large suitcase and pushchair and Michael in his new blue shirt and navy trousers, which I had bought in Wembley.

Uncle Dick blew alcohol in my face as he kissed me, and he said I was welcome to stay, as his work kept his wife Babs and her mother alone a lot.

The farmhouse was down a country lane, where we passed cow sheds leading on to a very large, very dusty and unkempt dwelling. Babs welcomed me, just as their boy, also called Michael and six years old, was on his way out to the cowsheds with a stick in his hand. "He loves to drive the cows in with the men," Babs said, and in we moved.

The weather was sunny and quite calm; the lane was full of blackberries. Babs' mother baked apple and blackberry pies and was always in the kitchen, which was vast in size, with flies on all the cups and plates on the dresser. She said it was always like it, and waved her hands to clear the flies off.

On Saturday she cooked sausage pie. I had never before seen plain pastry cut and put on a large dinner plate with skinned sausages then pressed into it and potato laid on top, well seasoned. She talked to me about their boy Michael, and said she was worried about Uncle Dick, who was unkind to him when he came home drunk.

I quickly learned that Uncle Dick was an alcoholic, and that he came home drunk and noisy most evenings. Not used to drink, I was upset and wrote to Rob and told him I was very unhappy and worried.

Air raids started now, both day and night. We all sat under a big wooden staircase. Quite often an unexploded bomb would be let off in a nearby field by an airman from the local Uxbridge aerodrome, and this would make us all jump. The farmhands sometimes would see this, and give us prior warning.

Rob wrote back to say he could get a weekend pass to come and take us to Gloucester, where he was stationed on a big airfield at Staverton. Among his duties there, he had to man a large anti-aircraft gun, which stood high up on a military vehicle.

He arrived on Saturday, the first time we had seen each other since 2nd July, the day he walked out to volunteer for the RAF. That night we all sat under the stairs from 9 p.m. until the early hours. Then Rob put a pillow down on the hearthrug. I asked him why he didn't come to bed with me. He replied that he was used to sleeping rough and preferred to be on his own. I slept until about seven, and found Rob was already up and shaved.

I had bought a large cabin trunk in Uxbridge for £1, so as to travel more easily. In it I packed all our things, including my one small ovenware glass casserole dish, which I'd had since 1936. It had a tray top and a deep base. I still have and use this base today in 1998. It cooked our stews every week.

Rob said everyone was able to go to bed and sleep in Gloucester, and he had got a temporary room for me and Michael in a cowman's cottage, in the grounds of Sir Gilbert McIlquham's farm.

We left Uxbridge that Sunday morning and arrived in London to find bomb debris everywhere. We picked our way over it to get to the tube to Paddington, where we had some food in the main station buffet. We arrived at Gloucester by mid-afternoon and got on the Cheltenham bus, which took us to Staverton. The cottage was reached by walking along a cow-field footpath, and on through a churchyard. There were three cottages all in a row. We stood outside 'our' cottage and knocked on the door, but no one was there. Rob tried the door and found it to be open, so we went inside and sat down. The inside of the cottage was small and dark, with a Kitchener stove alight and a kettle and a pot on the top.

Wanting the toilet, we found an outside privy with three seats side by side, well scrubbed but very smelly!

About 5 p.m. the woman returned. It was potato-lifting-and-bagging time. The cowman arrived home later. They were both very proud that Sir Gilbert had given them electricity recently, and showed me our room. This was reached by walking through their bedroom! The floors were wooden and slanted, as the place had subsided. Rob left for his camp, and went back to his tent on Staverton Airfield, which was opposite the Rotol Airscrews factory on the Gloucester-to-Cheltenham road.

The couple told me that the room was their son's. He was now in the army, and I could have it for three weeks. They advised me to walk to Longlevens and find a room there. It was about three miles away with country between. They told me Longlevens had shops and a post office, and the city of Gloucester was near.

After asking for a bath, I was shown a tin bath on a stone floor in an outside shed. A pitcher of hot water was given me, but it soon cooled on the stone floor.

The woman was out all day potato-picking, whilst the man came back at odd times for bites to eat. The main meal was at night – mostly joints of tender meat, and lovely vegetables, all cooked on the new electric stove.

Bristol was being badly bombed, and at night, from their back garden, we could see the searchlights and red glows in the sky to the south.

Staverton had a few cottages in the lane and I was introduced to the grocer from the general shop and nearby friends. A teapot stood on the Kitchener, and tea was poured out and handed round, dark and stewed. An awful brew! I had to hand some to Michael, but he didn't drink it.

It was now well into October, and I walked to Longlevens across the cow field to the main road with Michael in his pushchair. The cows stared at us as we walked past them. I was told they were used to people using the path.

Reaching Longlevens, I knocked on several doors, but all the owners shook their heads and said no. I went into Mrs Cross's general shop and asked if she knew of any rooms. A tall lady who was a customer standing behind me said, with a very broad Geordie accent, "You won't get anywhere with him," pointing at Michael. I told her I was very worried as the situation seemed hopeless, and it was the bombings in London that had driven us out, and our lodgings in Staverton were only temporary.

As I went towards the shop door, the lady called out, "I know your problem: I had three in the 1914 war, and had to come south to live. If you don't find anywhere, I'm Mrs Blair. I live at Challabrook in Longlevens Lane."

I thanked her and said I was Gladys.

After another week with no success, and only days away from having to move out, we walked back over to Longlevens and knocked on the door of Challabrook. There was no answer, so we went round to the back door and found it unlocked. I opened it and called out "Cooee!"

A voice replied from the landing, "Is that you, Gladys?"

I called back, "Yes," and I was told to come upstairs.

Mrs Blair was ill, and she said I was her 'blessing' that day. Would I please cook the dinner of meat and vegetables for her son and daughter, who would be coming in at one o'clock? I looked round and found a rather scruffy kitchen and stove, but got on with getting the dinner.

Bob, nineteen, came in from the Shire Hall, tall and very cheerful, saying, "Mum has got one of her turns again." Then Peggy (Peg) came in from school. She was seventeen. I put a dinner on a tray and Peg took it up the stairs to her mother, then we all sat in the dining room, ate our meal and chatted.

Around two o'clock, Mr Blair came in. He was the manager of Bon Marche's men's department, and it was his half-day. I got up and said we would go out and continue to find a room. We went towards Oxstalls Lane, where big houses were, but without any success. Some people were very sympathetic. However, there were no vacant rooms for me and a child.

Returning to Challabrook in the fading light, Mrs Blair was by the fire in her dressing gown, and Mr Blair was pouring tea. Mrs Blair said she and Mr Blair had discussed it and we could stay if I didn't mind sleeping with Peg. She took both of us upstairs, where there was an unmade bed.

Michael was three years old in another two weeks. He was very observant and full of talk. "I'm not sleeping there –" he said, "the blankets are dirty."

Mrs Blair said, "That is their colour, and they are quite clean."

I was so embarrassed, but she laughed and said he was a cheeky boy.

We quickly settled in with this happy family. Peg and I cleaned the house on Saturdays. The hall had a coloured tiled floor and no mat, I remember it well.

Mrs Blair was a very good cook, but she hated doing the washing and all housework. Half the dirty washing got put back in the cupboard, so Michael's observations were spot-on. However, Mr Blair's collars, Van Heusen, were all specially dried and ironed. "Dad is very particular in his job, and keeps tidy." Mrs Blair told me to iron them, then put them standing up on the piano top.

Mr Blair came home one day with a large black enamel saucepan, saying it was 10/-. Bon Marche had had a few delivered. I asked if I could have one, and I was lucky. All through the war, and long afterwards, it boiled all our white cottons and handkerchiefs, as well as jam being made in it. It was solid and heavy.

Everything Michael did or said was watched by Bob, who was full of fun, and Michael acted up to it all, especially at mealtimes. I wasn't strict, but I had no control over this.

In the meantime, I wrote off to London for extra money being offered to servicemen's families if bombs had caused them to move, and I was awarded 8/- extra a week.

Rob came to see us very often on his days off. He was able to get a sleeping-out pass, but at the Blairs', couldn't use it. One day, he heard about an estate built by Rotol Airscrews at Churchdown, for their workers to rent. There was country all around the estate and no houses except for a few large ones in Parton Lane.

The residents on this estate had mostly reserved occupations at Rotol, but some did have serving husbands and let rooms.

Rob saw a large room advertised on a board, so we went over on the bus and met a nice lady, Lucy King, who showed us a room that had a double bed, a nice suite, two armchairs, a dining table with chairs and a cupboard. It was big, and had a single-bar electric fire on the wall. The rent was just 9/- a week, so we took it.

The Blairs were pleased we could be together, and said we could come up any time and visit them.

I was so thankful to be, at long last, settled, and Churchdown was lovely. An hourly bus from the top of Parton Lane took us to either Gloucester or Cheltenham, and I had the use of Mrs King's kitchen for cooking and washing day.

Mr King worked at Rotol Airscrews, and he and his wife had their bedroom in the downstairs front room, under ours. They were both in their thirties and had a baby, eight months old. When I saw him, I was surprised that he lay inert, and never kicked or behaved as a normal baby behaved or acted.

Michael was lively and interested in everything at three years and he was never still.

Mrs Blair sent Bob over to invite Michael and me for Christmas Day. Rob was on duty, so I was pleased to accept.

Until we arrived, I didn't know that all she could get for Christmas dinner was a rabbit! I don't believe either she or Mr Blair had any of it, but plates were full of roast potatoes, swede, Brussels sprouts and a good thick gravy. This was followed by Christmas pudding and Mrs Blair's lovely home-made mince pies.

Afterwards we sang carols, with Bob playing the piano, and we finished by singing 'Bless This House'.

I walked miles with Michael, down the country lanes and footpaths around Churchdown, letting him toddle. He had one good coat and cord leggings, otherwise only a knitted outfit, which was a bit babyish for a three-year-old.

Being fairly close to Rotol Airscrews and Staverton Airfield, oil drums were placed in our streets, then lit up to form a smoke barrier and hide our estate. The smell was awful, and the pavements oily. Of course Michael slipped over and covered his clothes with crude oil. I had to take them to the cleaners in Gloucester, so he was forced to wear his pale-blue knitted woollen suit whilst they were being cleaned.

Michael played on the green outside the house, with the little girl next door and one day came in screaming and rubbing his eyes. "Beryl threw sand at me," he yelled.

I took him straight to the chemist near us. They gave me drops, saying the sand would work itself out of his eyes, but next morning his eyes were closed and swollen, so I took him on the bus to Gloucester Infirmary. A doctor there told me it was sand and lime, and I should have brought him yesterday. They washed out his eyes and strictly told me he could have been blinded – but he was all right, thank God.

After Christmas, the weather turned bitterly cold, and it snowed heavily, so we did not go out for several days. Michael was very good, and we read and recited nursery rhymes. His favourite story was 'The Three Bears'. I used to take off the voices of father, mother and baby bear. Michael would laugh and say, "'Gain, Mummy," until I was sick of it! He had a rag book, which I used to wash and then iron.

One freezing day, a small open lorry stopped outside, with soldiers standing in the rear of it. When the driver's door opened, I was amazed to see Joe jump down. Rob's brother told me he was now stationed in Stroud, and had been detailed to take the men on a routine drive and gun practice, so he thought he would come to Churchdown to see us.

Mrs King made a big enamel jug full of cocoa, and took it out to the very cold and grateful men, who all cheered her, with a hip-hip-hooray. It was a wonderful surprise, and it was so lovely to see Joe again.

When days were dry, I would push Michael in his pushchair into Churchdown village, then across the main railway line and walk the uphill road to Chosen Hill, a landmark some 500 feet above sea level. It was a lovely place to look down on Rob's airfield, and on towards Coombe Hill. Later on in the spring and summer, white and mauve violets grew all around and in August there were lovely large blackberries. I had never seen such large early ones before, and I made jelly with the rationed sugar I had saved up. We didn't take sugar in our tea.

Right on top of Chosen Hill, stands the small twelfth-century church of St Bartholomew, with the steep footpath so difficult to climb when wet and muddy. One day, I saw a funeral party, with the coffin being pulled up the path on strong wide cords. I used to wonder how many people walked so far, and climbed such paths, to go to church. I was told the villagers did.

Coming in one afternoon, I found Mrs King on her knees, pulling Kenny up by his arms on the fireplace rug. He was now a year old, and her mother had come to visit them from the Forest of Dean, where they had a farm.

"Mother says I must give Kenny exercise; he is very backward, and should be sitting up," she told me.

I thought Kenny had a lot wrong – he never chattered or smiled, but I never said so. Mrs King was sure he was very backward, and she called him 'a lazy boy'.

Eventually she took him to the village doctor, who said he was spastic. She refused to believe him and rang her mother, who told her to rub snails into his back. Folk remedies were still being commonly practised in rural country homes.

Finally, I helped her carry this now heavy boy to see specialists at the hospital. Sadly they could only confirm the doctor's earlier diagnosis.

Kenny only sucked milk, and Mrs King was fortunate enough to get plenty from Pirton Farm. I daily crossed the fields to the farm, to buy eggs, cheese and milk. The farmer's wife was very kind, and also gave me cucumber, beetroot and fruit.

The son also brought milk round to our doors, and at Christmas left cream – what a treat! – to go with baked apples or apple pie. They had beautiful peacocks strutting around outside their farmhouse. I was thrilled when the male displayed his lovely feathers.

When Rob was off duty and with us, he made Michael a truckle bed, to fold and put underneath my bed. I bought a mattress in Bon Marche, also a lovely velour pink dressing gown in the children's department, for myself, for 7/6d. I was only seven stone, and five foot three, so teenager-size.

I became friendly with the couple next door – Ashley and Kibby

Ellis. Kibby was thirty-five, Ashley forty and too old for call-up. They had a huge garden, full of vegetables. The soil was sandy and fertile.

When Kibby's sister came over in the morning, she would make a plateful of bread, margarine and jam and cups of tea. She often asked me round to join in with their chats and fun.

Kibby was a volunteer ambulance driver, in Gloucester. She was plump, small, with permed short curls and smoked heavily. She was full of life and laughter, and a joy to be with.

Ashley was the opposite – very quiet, but very pleasant to talk to. He worked in the office at Rotol Airscrews, and came home for dinner. His face was always serious as he walked in, but Kibby soon brought out his hidden sense of humour.

They both came from Yorkshire, and included many of their Yorkshire dialect phrases in their conversations, all of which I now forget.

Rob took to both of them, which started up us playing bridge on long evenings, and continued even after we moved again and until I finally left Gloucester in 1944.

I was enjoying my life at the Kings', and we got on well. Spring came, and all around cowslips bloomed. But there was an east wind blowing every day, and it was cold for Michael in his pushchair. I walked too far for his little legs, only giving him short walks, with him pleadingly asking, "How much further, Mummy?" He was now three and a half.

I picked cowslips as the cuckoo flew about us, and took them home. I packed them in cardboard, to send off to my relations in London and Surrey, and received warm thanks, as they didn't bloom there.

When we came back from one of our walks one day in late May, Mrs King said they needed my room. Kenny woke a lot in the night, and Mr King needed his sleep.

I went to get my pension at the village post office, and asked the assistant if she knew of any rooms to let. She said she lodged with the wife of an army man, who had two rooms she wanted to let for twelve shillings. She told me to go to Holtham Avenue right away.

Betty Richardson was about my age, and had a little son, nine months old.

The two rooms were her best ones: front top bedroom with a feather bed, and a very comfortable 'best room' underneath. Betty

Bull, the assistant from the post office, rented the small bedroom, and lived in with Betty Richardson and Paul.

We discussed her rules: by midday we had to be out of her kitchen, and, every other week, it would be my turn to clean the landing, stairs and hall.

I left the Kings' in a warm friendly way, and they were so very pleased that I now had two rooms.

Life with Betty was home from home. Washing day was lovely, with a copper, a rubber wringer, a long wire washing line, and clean country air – not London's smoke and fog.

The copper water was kept, to use with wire wool to clean the cooker – again every fortnight. This was a task for me to do.

Kibby and Ashley came once a week for bridge, with Michael tucked up in bed. He would never wake once he was asleep, and during the day was a quiet little boy, who played with his toys, some of which were home-made.

Rob had a bike, and Betty had one she readily lent to me. So, that summer, with a cushion on Rob's crossbar for Michael to sit on, we explored the Gloucester countryside.

Our favourite spot to visit was Wainlode Hill on the River Severn, where Rob could fish, and we would have a picnic, which I carried on the front of my handlebars. At other times, we would hire a rowing boat for a trip up the river. The war in those few hours would seem a thousand miles away.

One awful day, when returning, Rob was freewheeling at speed down a hill when Mike's feet got caught up in the front spokes of the bike, throwing them both off into the road. To my horror, both of Michael's ankles were badly cut, and I ran to a nearby cottage. The people inside were very kind, and bathed his feet in a bowl on the floor of their front parlour, advising me to take him to a doctor.

We cycled home – a long ride – and I took him straight to the village doctor. He dressed both ankles, and told me to keep him in a pushchair (if we went out) for a week, and not let him walk. Both ankles healed up very well, and Michael was soon running around again.

Round in Parton Lane I talked to a nice lady who sold eggs from her hens. I used to buy six from her every week. In a nearby lane, in a shed, an old man sold greengrocery, a lot of which he grew on his own land. I ate apples I had never heard of – Tom Putt was one – and big Bramleys.

At the end of Parton Lane, which was quite near, was a good butcher's where I could get liver, hearts, sweetbreads and cuts of meat for my casseroles. Michael and I would eat our dinner in Betty's dining room at twelve o'clock each day.

On Fridays the fishmonger called, and I remember him having plaice and gurnets as his specials. For my groceries, once a week I would walk to a tiny shop in the village. Sometimes I took the bus to Cheltenham, which I loved; or Gloucester, where we would meet Mrs Blair. We had coffee at the Cadena in Eastgate Street, and had a good long chat before going on to see Mr Blair in the Bon Marche.

I had been with Betty for over a year, when Reg, her husband, came home on leave. He told me his mother would have to come and live there, as his father had died. Both he and Betty were really sorry for me.

Betty Bull, now married, was able to stay on, as her husband was serving abroad.

The next-door neighbour told me to go opposite, as the wife had walked out with the little girl, and the man was alone now and needed a lodger. He only had his own bedroom furniture, a large sideboard and a dining-room table with chairs. The wife had taken the rest of the home with her. It was 'a little palace', I was told.

I spoke to Rob, who said straight away, "No!" He wouldn't hear of such a thing. However, the neighbour told us the man worked in the Rotol Airscrews offices and seemed nice. So Rob strolled over in the evening and came back later clutching a lettuce and a few baby outdoor marrows. Rob said he was a very nice chap, and we could get our own home down from London, and look after him for free. He wanted me to be his housekeeper.

Michael, now four and a half, was going to school in Parton Lane, in the church hall. I cleaned this hall for months for 10/- a week. The WRAF from Innsworth Lane used it for dancing every night, leaving it dirty and not fit for the infant school, who used it each following day. I knew the vicar, and he couldn't get anyone to clean it and said he would be most grateful if I could do it. I thought 10/- was worth having.

I would take Michael round with me, put him in a side room to play, and then I would sprinkle tea leaves over the floorboards and sweep this large hall thoroughly. After that, I had to clean the two toilets, and then scrupulously wash the large enamel pitcher, for the children's unpasteurised farm milk.

The children sat on long wooden forms, but I took Michael's own little chair for him to sit on, and he loved it there.

One morning, I woke with a terrible throat, and Betty called the doctor. I had tonsillitis and pharyngitis, and was very ill.

Whilst recovering, I was able to dwell on the most pleasant thoughts: that soon I would have my own home once more, and I would still be near to all my new Gloucester friends.

My home arrived in a van, from London, and we moved into 18 Holtham Avenue, with its long garden, which I could work in, and Michael could play in. It was so wonderful to have my own bed and furniture again that I danced an impromptu jig in Mr Wood's front room, whirling Michael round and round in sheer delight.

Rob was still stationed at Staverton, defending the enlarging airfield. On it, he set traps to catch wild rabbits, bringing me one or two each time he came home. The ones I didn't use, I would sell to eager buyers for 1/6d.

I learned how to skin and cut up a rabbit. It made a lovely stew, and, with half the remaining stew, I would make a delicious rabbit pie, which Michael adored.

We ate well, the garden providing us with curly kale, small cauliflowers, peas, strawberries and raspberries. I grew all our potatoes, and learned how to grow Brussels sprouts and brassica properly – stamping the ground when I planted my seedlings.

Michael made friends with both neighbours' little girls, who were the same age as him, as well as the little girl from across the road. All the families in the road worked at Rotol's, and ran cars, but they were all very nice and ordinary.

Their wages were very good and, to me, so were their hours. I had been used to evenings alone for four years, and it was only Wednesdays that Rob would come home early at 7 p.m. This was because it was the office girls' half day, so the salesmen finished early. I was a bit envious of my neighbours' good luck – exempt from service. But at least my life was settled now, and happy.

CHAPTER EIGHT

One afternoon, two cars came into our quiet road, and a man knocked on my door. The other man sat outside in the other car. He said he was from Blundells in Gloucester, and he wanted customers to buy on credit (1/- in the pound), to pay weekly for clothes, furniture, household goods, carpets and rugs.

I looked at him – his face was familiar. I said I thought I knew him, and asked his name. He said George Turner. I said my husband had worked for Bon Marche in Harlesden. He jumped and said, "Rob? Where is he?" I told him that Rob was stationed at Staverton and was able to come home often. George told me he had moved from London, having left his wife after twenty years of marriage, and was now the new manager of Blundells.

He then introduced me to the man sitting outside in his car. His name was Ray Pope. He said Ray was exempt from service – he was a smashing chap, and he was lucky to have him. Ray would collect all money in the area, once a week.

I needed a lot of things, and I had enough money now, so I ordered a long runner for the hall, a bedspread and some sheets.

Ray began to call each week to collect the money. He was very polite, and, some weeks later, I saw him eating his sandwiches in the car, so I asked him next week if he would like to come in and have them with a cup of tea. He said he would.

At this time, I had a girl of nineteen staying as a lodger. She was also a worker at Rotol's, and came home for dinner at one o'clock. Her name was Hester. She was a rather shy country girl. This arrangement suited Rob, who was relieved to know I wasn't alone at night with Mr Wood. His mother and sister, who lived in Devizes, came to visit, and they were so grateful I was looking after Mr Wood that they invited Rob and me to visit them, which we did when Rob had a free day. They gave us a nice dinner.

George Turner brought Mae to me, saying she was Mae Murray, and did all the Blundells office work. Rob and I visited George and Mae, at their flat over the shop, and they would come to us for tea. Mae told me one day that she had a son of eleven, who was very much missing her, but staying with a friend in London. George had refused to have him, but as she loved George, she had to accept it.

I had a put-you-up, and I said to Mae that I would take the boy. It meant a lot more work for me, as I already washed and boiled eight sheets on a Monday, but I was young and I could work all day.

I liked Mae a lot, and I was happy to help her. I don't remember his name, but he was a nice boy, and he made his bed himself.

Rob was moved from Staverton to a place in Warwickshire. When I wrote to him, I told him that my Aunty May lived at Long Buckby with her four children.

She had married Uncle Albert West, and subsequently had gone out to live in Montreal, Canada in 1923. Doreen was born in 1924 at Virginia, and she was called Doreen Virginia West.

Aunty was very unhappy out there, and after Anthony was born she came back with her two children, to live in England for good, leaving Uncle Albert behind.

Apparently, on renting a small cottage in Long Buckby, some few years later she met a countryman, and Shirley was born, then Ursula. But for some reason the countryman walked out on her, never to be seen again.

Without any money coming in now, she appealed to her brother, my Uncle Vic, and he sent her money for many years. He lodged with his brother, Uncle Sid, and his wife Nelly.

Rob cycled over to Long Buckby, and spent a day with them. Not knowing that I now had Mae's son, he told Aunty to let the three girls come and stay for a fortnight with me.

So a few weeks later I met my cousins on Gloucester Station, when Hester was on holiday, and I hadn't got Mae's son any more. He didn't like Gloucester, so Mae took him back to London.

Doreen was seventeen, blonde and very self-possessed; Shirley was thirteen, very moody and awkward; and Ursula was eleven and missing her mother after only one day. She looked at the clock at 5.30, and said, "Momma is coming up the lane from work now."

Rob had written to me and said he found a very happy family in a poor but spotless home. They were all singing when he knocked on their door – not aware they had a caller.

Next day, I took the girls on the bus to Cheltenham. Mike was at school. I showed them the lovely Prom, and we looked round the shops. Then as our bus was due to leave, Shirley absolutely refused to move from W. H. Smith's newspaper counter. Doreen begged her not to be difficult, and said, "I shan't take you anywhere again," and then told me, "She's in one of her moods – she gets like this."

We got home eventually, and we spent the rest of their stay in and around the Churchdown countryside and up on Chosen Hill. It was after Easter, and the days were now warmer.

On Saturday, I asked Doreen if she would like to go to the RAF dance at the church hall. I took her and stayed a while, then left her and told her to be home by ten o'clock. The small band had a microphone, and, after hearing Doreen singing, asked her to sing a solo. Her voice was lovely. I forget the song.

I walked back home, leaving her among WAAF girls, enjoying herself.

Ten o'clock came, then half past but no Doreen. I was so worried that I went round to the hall, to find it all shut up. I don't remember what time Doreen eventually came in, but I was very cross with her. She was in a happy mood, and said she had been for a walk with a nice American man, and found they had a lot in common with each other. Both were Roman Catholics.

Aunty May had married a Roman Catholic, became one herself, and brought up all her family in this faith.

Next day, Sunday, the three girls asked where their church was. Momma had said they must go as they always did. I told them that Gloucester was three and a half miles away, and there was no bus on a Sunday. Ursula said that Momma would be ever so cross, and she would have walked. Rightly or wrongly, I forbade it. They were all my responsibility and I liked to be with them if I could, but not all that way there and back.

I enjoyed the two weeks they spent with me, and saw them off at Gloucester Station.

Doreen told me that at home they were friendly with Tony Lowry, a pianist on the BBC and in well-known places. He played duets on two pianos with Clive Richardson, and a few years later we saw them playing with Mantovani's orchestra at the BBC theatre in London.

Tony Lowry wanted to have Doreen coached for a singing career, but I don't know if Aunty refused, or if Doreen did, but it never happened.

In 1946, Tony composed a song called 'Doreen'. It was a nice piano composition, and he played it at the Mantovani concert. I still have the sheet music and have played it often.

Ray came for his tea and sandwiches for a year. We always addressed each other as Mrs Riches and Mr Pope. I was twenty-seven, and Ray was twenty-four. It was quite normal to be formal in those days, as Christian names then were only for family.

One day, with Hester home for dinner, liking Ray and thinking Hester needed a boyfriend, I asked Ray if he went to the pictures. When he replied, "Yes," I said, "Why don't you take Hester?"

He smiled, she blushed a little, but nothing was said.

When I went to let Ray out the door, he turned to me and said, "I don't want to go to the pictures with Hester, but I wouldn't mind taking you."

I said I couldn't go out in the evening anyway, and I hadn't been to the pictures for years.

He said, "What about 2 p.m. on my half day?"

I was so tempted, that I said, "Yes, I will go."

The following week, we met outside the cinema, and Ray put a box of chocolates in my hand.

"How ever did you get these?" I asked. Sweets were rationed, and we were only allowed two ounces per head each week.

"Oh, Mam gets our sweets," Ray said. "I have two sisters and a brother, so we get plenty." His mother thought he had a new girlfriend.

Ray put his arm round me, and later kissed me. It moved me deeply. I was not in love with Rob – he never kissed or cuddled me. Our rare sex was over in moments, with a Rendells pessary inside me in case I had a baby. I used to think it was a wife's duty – loving didn't come into it, and never had.

We parted outside at 4.30, and went home on the bus. I was changed for ever, and longed for next week, to see Ray again.

Ray now started to pop in at night, and then said he would come on Saturday evenings and stay for a while. Knowing he usually had his dinner at night, I saved things, and cooked him a meal with fresh potatoes and cabbage.

I was in love. We kissed a lot and we talked a lot. I asked him why he was not called up. He said he was afraid to tell me in case

I might not understand, and stop seeing him. Eventually he told me he was a committed Christian, and a conscientious objector. He had been passed by a military panel, unanimously. He was a very gentle boy, very kind in his whole manner – so different to my blunt often hard husband, who expected everything I did, as part of my obligation as a wife, and then criticised me over a lot that didn't come up to his expectation.

Ray's voice and kind ways, together with his marvellous sense of humour and spontaneous witty comments, were wonderful for me.

Stan Cole and Eva were in love and kissed often, but our marriage was very businesslike in comparison.

One Saturday, I was cooking a meal for Ray, who was sitting in a chair, when the back door opened, and Rob, with heavy kitbag, gas mask and rifle slung over his shoulder, came in.

He had met Ray, of course, but was furious to find him there. He ordered him to get out, and fingered his gun. Ray protested that he was just a friend, but Rob looked really evil.

Without any thought, I got my coat and said to Ray, "We will go to your house."

We left immediately. I never gave poor Michael a thought.

Rob was being moved to Lydd in Kent, to guard the coastline with his troop, so he had asked for leave and had managed to get two days.

Ray and I drove to Hucclecote, and found his mother and two sisters, Betty and Mary, sitting by the fire. Ray told his mother what had happened and how Rob had been, and said he had brought me home for a night.

Mrs Pope was a plump, homely mother. She asked us to come into the front room, shut the door, and quietly said to Ray, "Why didn't you tell me your girlfriend was married? I could have advised you."

She told Betty, the elder of the two sisters, to make up a bed in their room, on a single folding bed-chair. It was a cold, frosty night, and I lay awake all night, but had warm blankets over me.

In the morning, Mary got up and went downstairs, and Betty said, "Come into bed with me and get warm." She expressed sympathy, and told me she was divorced, had married when she was young and had made a big mistake. She was twenty-five and very friendly.

Downstairs, I found all the family at breakfast. Mrs Pope was slicing bread at a great pace, whilst the family were busy spreading jam on their cut slices and washing it down with hot cups of tea.

Mr Pope worked on the railway (GWR), and had been a driver on the Northern Express runs until a spark blinded him in one eye. His work was changed to shunting and his wages cut sharply. Although only in his early fifties, his hair was pure white. He looked at me severely, and he said, "You go back home to your husband, my girl."

Ray whispered later, "Don't let him worry you – he is very strict."

But he did worry me. I felt very lost among them all. Mary ignored me, whilst Ted, the younger brother, just looked at me, expressionless.

They had a lovely old dog, and he sat by me. It was bath day for all of them and they put on clean clothes. They had a bathroom upstairs and a lavatory outside, spotlessly clean, with cut up newspaper squares strung up on the wall.

The girls helped Mrs Pope cook the Sunday joint and vegetables, whilst Ray played Bing Crosby records. In the afternoon, Ray took me for a walk; it was cold and sunny and, looking towards Chosen Hill, the countryside looked beautiful. At a field gate Ray kissed me and put a ring on my finger. It was a bow, set with diamonds. I had never had a ring of any value.

The month after Rob and I had decided to marry, I had bought myself a ring for £1, with a fake stone in gold, to look engaged. Rob didn't believe in engagements, but I showed it off to Kath and Gilly when I was working at the music shop in 1935. The stone fell out soon afterwards.

Going back to tea, Betty saw the ring and said, "You have got my ring," but Ray said, "It is mine – I bought it from you, didn't I?"

No more was said.

I stayed with them for a further night, but I was worrying about Michael, so I decided to go back home early next morning.

I told Ray not to come for a few days, and knew inside of me that Mr Pope was right – it was all wrong.

Upon returning to Churchdown, I found that my neighbour was looking after Michael, who had coolly told her, "My mummy has run away," then played with her little girl unconcernedly. The neighbour was nice and very sympathetic about it all.

Kibby came round, and I told her about what happened at the weekend. She was very practical with her opinion, saying, "Ray is single, and he will find another girl. You must part from him."

I wrote a letter to Ray, and told him we must stop seeing each other and, from now on, I would pay for my goods at the shop in town.

George and Mae said I could carry on, in their opinion, but not let Rob know. But I couldn't lead a double life, so I just got on with my daily tasks.

However, the following Saturday night as I sat by the fire, the back door opened and Ray came in. We hugged and he told me he had done his rounds up at Hereford, with me on his mind all the week. He had told his parents that he would find lodgings there, but, when it came to it, he couldn't do it, as he wanted me so much.

I wanted him too, with a new desperate and deep love. We knew now that we must be together, and so he stayed.

When Mr Wood came home, we told him what we had decided. He stood against the wall and said, "What goes on behind this bloody wallpaper is your business in this bloody place." I thought he would tell me to go, but he continued, "Your lives are your own – work it out." Then he sat down to eat his dinner and his beloved rice pudding, before going back out again.

I wrote to Rob, now at Lydd, and said I wanted a divorce, and Ray moved in with me.

Rob came as soon as he could get some compassionate leave, and told me that if I was in love with Ray, we must find our own place and divide the home up.

As we were deciding upon this, Rob suddenly said, "I won't find anyone else to keep my washing as white as you do." It was an unexpected tribute, and surprised me greatly. He said he would arrange to store the furniture in Gloucester.

Next day I went round and told Mrs King about Ray, and that Michael most probably would be taken away from me by Rob. She said, "No one has ever fed and cuddled Kenny besides myself," adding, "Are you sure you are doing the right thing doing this?"

Then came the time to tell Mrs Blair. She wasn't at all surprised, and said she had seen Rob's attitude towards me and deserved to lose me. "He's a dog in a manger, in my opinion," she said.

On Easter Sunday 1944, Ray, myself and Michael travelled from Gloucester to my parents, who lived in Carshalton, Surrey, so that we could have a meeting and discussion. When we arrived, they greeted us warmly. My mother was lucid and in a normal frame of mind, which was sweet and kind.

While Mother made some tea, Ray, Michael and I sat with my father in the drawing room. My father told Ray he was pleased we had met, and that he had never been happy about my marriage. He said he felt that Rob was not right for me, although he admitted that he seemed to have improved lately, but he knew I wasn't happy.

That night Evelyn was conceived in the little room of their lovely house, and she was born nine months later, a week overdue, on 11th January 1945, at St Michael's Hill Nursing Home in Bristol. It was a frosty then snowy night. She weighed 7lb 12oz, and she was perfect, like a doll with black hair. It was an almost painless birth.

Ray and I returned to Gloucester, leaving Michael with my parents. We set about finding somewhere to live, and managed to find two rooms in the city of Gloucester, with a nice lady; and so we started on, we hoped, a happy life together.

The lady was Miss Gingell, and she had her brother with his bedridden wife living with her.

She owned a row of houses, which her father had left her, and the rents she got from them were her only income.

I had the use of the kitchen for washing day, ironing, and cooking the evening meal.

Ray felt compelled to change his job, and became an insurance collector, working in and around the Forest of Dean. I often came with him on his rounds in his Morris 8 car, and we discovered coal miners and forest people living lovely simple lives.

A lot of families kept a pig on their plot and they gave Ray some pieces for me to render down for dripping, which I used to make pastry.

During late spring and early summer, we were given cherries and strawberries, and sometimes I was invited into their homes for a cup of tea. I have very fond memories of the forest in 1944.

Among the trees we saw huge piles of army supplies and coloured American soldiers with guns, standing on guard on the roadside.

Neither of us knew then that this was the build-up for D-Day and the final invasion of the war to free Europe from Hitler. The hidden supplies were later driven to the docks in Bristol, for onward shipment to the disembarking troops at Normandy.

One evening, after returning from a day out in the forest, I sensed a strange change in Miss Gingell's attitude towards us. I had brought back a large bunch of foxgloves, to put in a pot in the fireplace for each of us.

She said, "Wash your hands – they are poisonous," then, "I have received a letter telling me you are not married – is this true?"

I replied that we were not, and I expected her to tell us to go!

However, Miss Gingell said that she had discussed it with her brother and decided we could stay. She liked us both, and, as far as she was concerned, it didn't matter.

Ray had his suspicions who the letter was from, as that person wasn't in agreement about us being together. The rest of the family were kind to me, and his parents hoped we would marry later on. Mrs Pope was kind and very generous and always had a 'tin storage' for us, which we were pleased to have.

One day Ray visited George Turner and was offered a job back with Blundells, but down in Bristol, thirty miles away. Ray said he would think about it.

We had had a blissful time at Miss Gingell's, and I loved my happy life. Ray and I sometimes went to Evesham on the river – both of us could row a boat, or enjoying lovely long country walks, smiling and laughing at the silliest of things.

We always went to church on Sundays. Ray was a lay preacher at some of the churches, and Baptist church services were different to my Presbyterian ones. I learned new hymns, and I saw baptisms (being submerged in water) for quite a few people. The bath was under boards, which were removed for the baptisms.

I had been to Church of England evensongs with Hester at Hatherley. I liked these very much, and came out afterwards feeling very happy.

Now religion began to puzzle me, and particularly chapel in the rural villages. However, I was happy to go to church with the man I loved. He was so natural, always cheerful and witty, that I knew he was a genuine and committed Christian. We didn't discuss religion very much, but in the pulpit he was very interesting, and his sermons were never too long. I knew he was a good preacher.

His sister Betty told me that he used to put a piece of drapery over his shoulder when he was a boy, and make the three of them his congregation.

Mr and Mrs Pope were Baptists, and went to the evening service in Northgate Street in Gloucester. We all went together one Sunday, and the minister spoke about children. He said mothers were more important in bringing them up and giving them security. He was a father himself.

This seemed to be directed towards me, and I became determined to have Michael back as soon as it became possible. But I was pregnant, and I knew that I could provide no home for him at this present time.

Ray decided to accept the Blundells offer, and was given the job immediately. He travelled from Gloucester to Bristol for quite a time, then one day said he had found a flat in Bristol's City Road.

So we left Miss Gingell and moved to a big old house owned by a Mr and Mrs Davidge. Mrs Davidge was sixty, and she told Ray she would love another baby and would be willing to look after it if I went out to work. I told Ray that would never be, and he agreed.

I was now being very sick all day and feeling very poorly, so I arrived looking ghastly.

Mrs Davidge said, "You go to bed, my dear," and to Ray, "Don't worry – she will be all right."

It was summer, very hot and almost a heatwave. I found myself in an old place with an ancient oven which didn't cook and I was in the centre of Bristol with no garden or flowers. I was totally bewildered and feeling very unwell.

Mrs Davidge had a thirteen-year-old daughter called Evelyn. She proudly told me she was forty-six when she had her, and she said she was very precious.

I thought, in 1944, that Evelyn sounded so nice, that if I had a girl, I would call her Evelyn too – and I did!

Ray quickly realised he had not found the right place for me, but learned of a railwayman called Dicks, who knew Mr Pope. Mr Dicks and his wife lived at Knowle, a nice area in the south-west suburbs of Bristol, and they were able to offer us two rooms: one up and one down.

We were happy here, and made plans to save for our own home. Houses to let then were quite easily obtainable.

One morning in early autumn, a letter came from Rob. He was now stationed in Wiltshire, and he was expecting to be sent abroad soon. He said we had to meet to discuss things, and I could say to the Dicks that he was my brother.

Several days later, Rob arrived with his girlfriend, Roberta (Bobby), and he was in cheerful mood. He told me that Michael was now at a grammar school in Wallington, and that my mother worshipped him.

Bobby lived with her father, and Rob stayed with them whenever he got leave, so he wanted us to get divorced. He said he wanted several photos, and that he could get the divorce done through the RAF.

The law in 1944 took away any children from a deserting wife, so I knew I had no chance to have Michael. I missed him dreadfully and had a deep conscience that I had disrupted his life.

However, the months passed by, and Ray and I were very happy and had settled in well at Knowle.

Rob had decided that Michael should live with him and Bobby during schooltime, and in the holidays he could stay with me and Ray. But without a proper home and in war I felt it was all wrong.

I asked a nursing sister at the antenatal clinic, if there was anyone I could consult for advice. She told me to go to the 'Women's Aid' in the Bristol Centre.

There, a chain-smoking head adviser said it would be best to give my baby to a well-off childless couple, and take back Michael; mixed marriages didn't work. This opinion was also my father's, in a letter written to me in confidence (my mother didn't know). So I agreed, and later that day told Ray.

He said he would care for me until I was free to go up to Surrey, to be reunited with Michael. Rob was now abroad in Belgium, but he knew my plans.

Evelyn was born on 11th January 1945, and, just a few days later, a lady and man, whom I never saw, came and collected her.

Mrs Pope and Betty came immediately after the birth to see and to hold her – they never once criticised me.

The day Evelyn went the snow lay dry and crisp, and the cotoneaster under my window sparkled with frost. I felt dreadful and cried uncontrollably.

Ray later came and took me to a Mrs Powell, who was young with two small children. Her husband was in the navy and she had been a bomb victim when she lived in Plymouth. She was so friendly and kind. Ray and I shared a bed and I stayed to get strong.

I received no advice about my abundance of milk, but the clinic took it daily for 'dry mothers' babies', then bound me tightly, and it eventually went.

I returned to Surrey and Briar End, and immediately took Michael to rooms I had found in Waddon, in the road where Stan Cole's parents lived. I was adamant about Mother's concern over Michael, and moved him to the local infant school.

We stayed there for several weeks, until I saw an advert in a Cheam local paper for someone looking for a 'service' mother and baby, to live in and be company.

I got a bus to Cheam, and found a nice house and a very friendly Gwen, so we happily and very swiftly moved in.

She had had cancer of the bowel, and had had a colostomy. Her son was the same age as Michael, and they got on together straight away.

Gwen's husband, Jack, soon started to kiss me, and I had to push him off – I didn't like him at all. But he played the piano, and gave me 'The Dream of Olwen', which was very popular in 1945, putting his signature on the front of the sheet music.

Talking to Gwen one morning, I said how sad I was. I had always wanted children but I had had to part with Evelyn. There was three months allowed for mothers to take their baby back, if they wished, and that length of time since Evelyn had been taken from me was almost up.

Gwen said, "Go and get her, Glad – she can come here."

She looked after Michael. He had changed his school once again, and now went to the local infant school in Cheam. I travelled back to Bristol and went to the 'Women's Aid'. The head adviser exploded when I said I wanted Evelyn back. She said that Evelyn was now Patricia, but, still very angry, she said she would ask the couple to bring her to me.

I waited, and when the lady arrived with Patricia (Patreeciar), I was shocked. She was very flashy, with cigarettes in an open costume pocket and a refined reedy voice. She wasn't at all upset, but just handed Evelyn over to me and drove off in a car.

I had written to Vera Powell, telling her of my intentions, and, with Evelyn in my arms, I stood waiting for a bus to take me to her at Staple Hill.

Bristol Centre at six o'clock in the evening was packed with lines of people queuing for their bus. I had no idea where Ray was now, but suddenly I saw him, pipe in mouth and reading his evening paper, standing in the Knowle bus queue.

We kissed, and then said he would come to Vera's with me. When we arrived, Vera took Evelyn from me, then hugged me and said there was a room, a cot and a bottle all ready for me to use – her daughter was now a toddler.

Ray left, but said he would return next afternoon and bring a low pram and take us to Weston-super-Mare, where his parents were on the 'Railway Early' holiday. It was April.

When he arrived next day with pram, a cuckoo cuckooed so clearly that Ray turned to me and said, "When you first hear the cuckoo, you will be in the same place next year." It was a country saying, but I didn't take it seriously then.

I had both my children now, and I knew I could work and keep them. I was used to poverty, and I wasn't afraid. I was thirty, and domestic work was needed in places like Cheam, and all of it was well paid.

None of this did I discuss with Ray, who never asked or said anything; but he wanted his mother to see Evelyn again, as she had been so upset at losing her.

After a short journey in the car to Weston, and a walk along the front, we found Mr and Mrs Pope, on a chilly afternoon, sitting in a shelter.

Dear Vera had given me warm blankets and lots of baby things, and, with Evelyn asleep in the pram, Mr Pope said we must come back with them to their lodgings, and stay the night with the train-driver friend they were staying with.

Mrs Pope was so happy once again to be able to hold and cradle Evelyn. She was so good and full of laughter, and she had two little dimples on her cheeks.

The friend gave Ray and me a single three-foot bed to sleep in, whilst Evelyn slept in her pram.

I prepared a bottle in their kitchen. She had Humanised Trufood, and added Adexolin – the food I was told she had been on with the lady she had lived with. It was expensive, but Ray paid for it willingly.

I got up at 4 a.m. to make another bottle and found the man drinking tea, before going off to work on the railway. He was very friendly, and told me I had a lovely baby.

In the morning, we discussed being together again sometime, and Ray said he would look out for an empty house in Bristol. Mrs Pope said Betty would help her get a home ready whenever Ray found one.

We returned to Bristol later that morning, and Ray put me on the train to Paddington, with the vow that he would come to see us if Gwen would agree. I said it was a long way to come. He said, "I'll come," and stood on the platform, waving me out of Temple Meads Station.

When I got back to Cheam, I found Gwen had prepared her large washing basket with blankets, and I laid Evelyn gently down in it, where she lay and kicked happily. Gwen's husband came in with the boys, and they gazed down with curiosity. I felt so very happy and grateful.

However, Gwen said that as the neighbours already knew me, I should tell them I was looking after a friend's baby – the boys too! Michael was seven and took no notice afterwards.

Gwen said Ray was welcome, and his parents too, as long as I fed them. The house was big, and so was Gwen's heart.

The weather turned very warm and I soon got domestic work, cleaning large houses in the area. I even worked on a Saturday morning, taking Michael with me to a big house by the Sutton cricket ground, and leaving him in one of the rooms to amuse himself, whilst I got on with cleaning the rest of the house.

VE day was announced on the radio and we all celebrated the news. At school Michael was given a bag of sweets and a printed message from King George VI, for being brave during the dark days of the war. Gwen's son said he didn't deserve it, as he had lived in Gloucester; but Michael had lived through bombings, disruption and the doodlebugs, and I felt he was entitled to it.

The two boys continued to get on with each other and would cycle off to Nonsuch Park and play in the large grounds there.

One hot day, Rob turned up to see Michael and to talk about things with me. He gave Michael 6d, and the boys went off to Nonsuch to buy an ice cream.

The war in the East was still going on, but Rob thought it only a matter of time before peace was restored to the whole world. His leave was brief and he returned to his unit, now out in Germany.

Then I heard from Ray, who said he had found a terraced house in Wells Street, Bedminster and that it would soon be ready for us to move into.

Mrs Pope, however, wasn't at all happy about its location, nor with the house itself, but Bristol had been very badly bombed and there were so few empty houses available. She, with daughter Betty, helped to make it habitable. It had just had some electricity installed downstairs, but gas mantles were everywhere else. There was a tiny yard at the back, with an outside lavatory; and there was no bathroom, but a tin bath hanging on the wall outside!

It was June when Ray arrived one Sunday in his car to fetch us. We left Cheam and an understanding Gwen, and set off for Bristol to start our new life together.

We drove past the famous White Horse in Wiltshire, and arrived to find that Mrs Pope, Betty and Mary had hung the curtains – the blackout was thankfully now over – and had made it look all very nice and clean. The living room was comfortable with a good fireplace, and Betty – bless her! – had lent us her household things and also her dining-room suite.

I wrote to Rob and said I intended to marry Ray – we had Michael with us and we were all well and happy.

Straight away, we bought a good second-hand upright pram for Evelyn, and had it reconditioned in dark crimson, with a new leather cover and new wheels. It really was warm and comfortable, and we kept it in the living room for her to sit and sleep in. Later we got a playpen and Evelyn was so contented and a complete joy for us.

The tiny kitchen had a stone floor, a built-in copper, a sink and a nice gas cooker. I made a good thick mat from sacks, to keep my feet warm.

So our happy life began. Michael went to the local council school, and told me, "Some of the boys' mothers don't care for them!" When I asked him what he meant, he said their clothes were dirty and some didn't have any shoes! But as always he made a friend – a poor little chap called Dicky.

Ray would sing, "Dicky-Dicky-Diney, shirt out behind 'e," and we called him Dicky Diney from then on.

Wells Street was close to the Bristol City football ground. At the back of our small yard was a passageway, which ran down to a public house on the main road. So the first August game brought men in droves, and, after going to the pub, to my horror, they urinated on the back of our wall. The lady next door, Mrs Ball, said quite cheerfully, "Oh, they do that other times too!" Her wall was a regular target also. The walls were about five feet high, but you could see their heads. I only used the yard for hanging my washing, and there was a line running down its short length.

One day I put Evelyn in her pram outside on the pavement for some fresh air. She was all clean with a white pillow and pink cover over her. Later I was shocked to find soot covering it all. This was yet another blow, and again there was an obvious reason

– Wills' Cigarette Factory was just round the corner, and this would happen whenever the wind blew in our direction. All the neighbours accepted such things with little concern. They had lived there for years, and had brought up their families there.

The Balls still had older children living at home with them, and Mary Ball, I was told, would be having a big twenty-first birthday party. I wondered where all the guests would go, as all the rooms were so small.

When the party took place, a piano was hired and put in their hall, adjoining our own. The noise all night was unbelievable. We had a long sleepless night and felt very annoyed, but next day she appeared with Mary, saying to Ray and me, "I expect you heard us having a good time – Mary loved it, didn't you, love?" and Mary gave just a half smile.

At the beginning of Wells Street was a small greengrocer and general shop, run by a cheerful lady, Mrs McCreedy. Very often she would keep things for me under the counter, and her beetroot was perfect. "Yes," she agreed, "Mr McCreedy grows the right sort for the winter – not many growers understand vegetables."

When Mrs Pope and Mary came to visit, Mrs Pope would enjoy a nice lettuce and say, "Where did you get this from, Gladys? It is so fresh."

I would say, "Mrs McCreedy's," and this remark became a regular household saying. But I did owe a lot to Mrs McCreedy, for my children's fresh and wholesome vegetables, as I had no ground in which to grow my own.

On the other side of the main road was Ashton Park. I used to walk through this with Evelyn in her pram, down to the River Avon towpath, with its grimy buildings along its banks. Boats came and went on it, with some stopping for the Wills' Cigarette Factory. Nothing in the Bedminster air was fresh – it always had a smell hanging over it. Ray said when the war was over we would move.

I found myself pregnant once again, and was delighted – two children so close in age, just like my sister Betty and me, would be, I hoped, such close companions for each other.

It was early August when my sister, Betty Wontner, came to stay with us. We managed to get a bed and a chest of drawers for her in the tiny third bedroom.

We took her to see the Clifton Suspension Bridge, before going on to Bristol Zoo, where we saw Alfred, the huge gorilla. He made us laugh by smoking cigarettes that people had pushed through the bars of his cage.

In the evening, we went to the Colston Hall and enjoyed seeing Hutch (Leslie Arthur Hutchinson) singing at his piano, with his characteristic mopping of his forehead with a white handkerchief, which he kept in his top pocket.

There were other artistes on the bill, and one of them had prizes to hand out to lucky members of the audience. They had to answer questions or produce odd things asked for. One such question was "Has anyone in the audience a large mole on their leg?" My sister immediately jumped up – she had one below her knee!

A normally shy girl, she went up to the platform, and came back with six thick white dinner plates. She thrust them at Ray and said, "I don't want them – they are too heavy for me." (I still have and use one of these plates, fifty-three years later!)

One night in mid-August, in bed, we heard boats hooting loudly on the Avon, and bells ringing continuously, waking us all up. People came outside our window shouting, "The war is over."

No one went to work next day, VJ day. We drove up to Gloucester after breakfast, to join all the family, and saw the beacons lit up on the Cotswold Hills all around Hucclecote.

Ray said Michael must do something to remember the day, and we drove off the main road to a small church with a graveyard and yew trees in it. Inside the church we found the bell ropes and Ray said, "Pull this hard, Mike," and in this quiet lane the bell rang out loudly all around.

After a few minutes, Ray said, "Let's go – someone may come." So we got back to the car quickly and drove off, laughing at this 'daring' act of celebration.

Telling Mrs Pope later, she said, "It had to be a church, didn't it, Ray?" and she laughed.

I had brought our meat and vegetables with us, and I helped Mother cook for her big family. The dining room had a large table, able to seat a dozen easily and everyone was happy. It was a good day.

The news later that an atomic bomb had wiped out whole cities of Japan, with complete destruction, was a shock. What was atomic? It was a new word to the man in the street.

We who were left could only reflect that we had survived a

dreadful war, and life could now get back to normal. I was thankful that my baby would be born in peacetime, and I was so very contented with life now.

Wells Street celebrated with a street party, with trestle tables down the middle of the road and bunting and flags flying from the top windows of the little terraced houses. The children tucked in to jelly and blancmange and home-made cakes and there was fun and laughter for everyone, finishing with a bag of chips for each child.

Later the tables were moved to one side, and the hokey-cokey was performed by my deliriously happy and noisy Wells Street neighbours.

Ray was a good father, and took Michael with him on Sunday mornings when he went out lay preaching at different churches in the Bristol area. He took him sometimes to the pictures, and on a Sunday afternoon he would take us out somewhere. It was really appreciated by me, as Sundays pre-war had meant keeping quiet for over two hours. Michael's nature was quiet, never boisterous, and he loved me to read to him. I had always loved the outdoors and walks and now they were enjoyed and loved by us all.

One lovely autumn afternoon, Ray said he had enough petrol (petrol permits were for work only) for us to go to Weston-super-Mare. We had a walk along the front, and then went into a tea shop owned by Charles Forte – recently opened, we were told. A waitress politely took our order – tea and cakes – and, when we finished, we paid Charles at his till.

Next day, Monday, our insurance man called as usual, and I went for my handbag. To my horror, there was the awful realisation that I had left it at Forte's. I had put it on the back of my chair when I had Evelyn sitting on my knees. The bag held our identification cards, ration books, insurance book, and Michael's RAF allowance book.

I put Evelyn in the pram, went to a phone box, and got Charles Forte's phone number from the operator. Charles answered my call and asked me to tell him the colour and size of my handbag, then told me that the waitress had given it to him after we left. He said he would post it to me.

Next morning it arrived. I was so grateful that I posted back a pound note with a letter of thanks.

Charles wrote back to tell me the waitress had refused any reward, and he had put it in his charity box.

How little I knew then that Charles Forte would become famous for catering, and that in the 1990s he would attempt to buy the Savoy in London, contested strongly by Sir Hugh Wontner, the Savoy managing director.

Hugh Wontner is connected to our family on the distaff side. His family name was Wontner-Smith, but his actor father, Arthur Wontner, dropped the name Smith.

Arthur Wontner famously played Sherlock Holmes in the 1930s, and featured in *Genevieve* towards the end of the film.

I corresponded regularly with Hugh, after my father's death in 1968. He became the Lord Mayor of London in 1976.

The autumn was mild, we enjoyed our outings, and we all kept well. I was carrying my baby well and had no sickness, as with Evelyn.

The days were full for me, and Ray helped at bedtime, settling the children. Our bath time was enjoyable – in front of the fire in the tin bath. The water was heated by the grey enamel gas copper in the kitchen, and afterwards we had to cart the bath outside, to pour the dirty water down the drain. There was always lots of fun between us, and Ray was so full of life. Afterwards, we had our cocoa and biscuits, and then went to bed.

In early November, Rob called and told us he had seen the RAF solicitor, and that he and his wife-to-be, Bobby, would have custody of Michael, except for school holidays, when I would have him. Michael was in the room with us and said nothing. I was very sad, but understood I couldn't have it all. I knew that Michael wouldn't have been alive if Rob had had his wish, and I strongly felt that he was mine.

Next morning I heard Michael crying – I thought he must be ill, as he was a very happy boy.

But he was very unhappy. He sobbed, "I don't want to live with Daddy and Aunty Bobby. I want to live with my mummy and daddy like we did." I was shocked and completely unsettled by his words. Michael was right – it was his life I had upset. I hadn't realised what the war had done to him, at two and a half years old, torn away from his natural family. I had no control over the war and bombs, but I would restore his future if I could. I got down on my knees and I prayed, "Please, God, help me, and show me what to do."

CHAPTER NINE

With my unborn growing baby I had been going down regularly to the antenatal clinic. After the nurse had examined me, I asked her if she could tell me where to go for advice; I told her I wasn't married and had a big problem. She was very kind and said I could go to the Welfare Centre and see a Mrs Stott.

I made an appointment over the phone, and I took Evelyn with me. I was shown where to sit and wait, and I expected to be told off over my circumstances, so I dreaded seeing Mrs Stott.

When I was called, I found a stout motherly lady with a smile, and she said, "Now, my dear, you can tell me all about your troubles."

So I poured it all out. I said right away that I was not in love with my husband, but I thought I should ask him to take me back for Michael's sake and future stability. I also said that I was pregnant, but hoped that Rob might take Evelyn and bring her up together with Michael, and perhaps I could have my unborn baby adopted by a childless couple.

Mrs Stott looked gravely at me and said, "If you and Mr Pope are in love, you will be doing an awful thing to him; but you are right to think about Michael. He is only seven, and your husband does have the right to him. I can't advise you, but I will help you when you really make up your mind. Come and see me then."

I went back to see her later and said I had put Michael first, and that I wanted to keep both my babies, but my husband didn't like children. I was very unhappy and afraid that he wouldn't take Evelyn, let alone my unborn child.

Mrs Stott listened intently and said, "Haven't you spoken to your mother about all this, dear?"

I told her that my mother was schizophrenic, and it was not

possible to discuss anything sensibly with her.

Mrs Stott said she was old enough to be my mother, and she would go and see my husband. I told her he was due out of the RAF sometime before Christmas, and he would be in Wiltshire with his girlfriend. Mrs Stott said she would get in touch with me later.

I wrote to Rob without telling Ray. I was now just so determined to break this wrong situation I had created for Michael. To add to my conviction, I went to Temple Meads Station one day and saw a man and a lady meet a boy from the train. He was carrying a large case, obviously from boarding school, and I watched them hug him and then they went off together happily.

I thought hard about this, and although I now knew life with Rob was unnatural in marriage, I was determined Michael was going to have both of his natural parents again. My feelings were not important.

Mrs Stott wrote to me and said she had seen Rob. She had told him I was a born mother with Michael and Evelyn, but I was willing to give the baby I was carrying to a childless couple. She said Rob was not keen to take Evelyn, but he was willing to take me back, and he agreed in the end.

I went to see Mrs Stott to arrange adoption, and she said I must leave Ray. She said she would arrange to get me in the Elm House shelter at Cotham Hill.

Ray was upset, but he said he always felt (as I did) that we had both done wrong.

He took Evelyn to Brights and had a lovely studio portrait of her taken, then told me his mother would care for her when I went into Elm House.

Mrs Pope was so kind to me, I felt ashamed I was letting Ray's family down, and causing so much heartache, yet Ray himself was understanding and kind about my decision.

Rob, now demobbed, took Michael back to London on the train for Christmas with his brother Joe and wife Gladys at Kingsbury, whilst Ray and I went to Hucclecote.

I was already very heavy, and in a maternity dress, but found Mrs Pope still the same as ever, the mother of her family, with the turkey in the oven.

Mary Pope had made an acquaintance with an Italian prisoner of war. His name was Eric, and he spoke very little English, but he was cheerful and a lovely guest to have at Christmas.

Presents from around the tree were given after lunch, and then we played simple games. One caused such fun and merriment: squeak, piggy, squeak, with one of us blindfolded and the rest in a circle round him.

When Eric's turn came, he said loudly, "Squeak, squeakity, squeak," in his rich Italian voice.

Mrs Pope said, "Eric, it is piggy."

He replied, "What is piggy?"

We all said, "Pork – we eat pork," but he just laughed – he was so happy to be with a family on Christmas Day.

After Christmas, I had to see Mrs Stott, and she said I could go now to Elm House. I told her I must do things for Ray first – wash and iron and clean up the house. He was going to stay there and get a woman to clean once a week. He liked his work and own independence.

I packed my trunk, and Ray took it, along with some bags in his car, to Elm House.

When he came back, he said, "I don't like you going there."

I asked, "Why?"

He said, "The lady in charge said there wasn't room for all that luggage, and she was old and sharply spoken," but he had left the trunk in a top attic.

I was expecting around late April, so I dreaded a sort of punishment spell with discipline, but I turned up one afternoon and Miss Vowles took me into a sitting room. There were girls sitting all around, and she asked one of them to take me up to my bed.

This girl said to Miss Vowles in a cross voice, "The water was cold when I had my bath," but Miss Vowles said nothing and marched off.

The girl took me upstairs and told me that everyone had to work in the mornings, and that Miss Vowles pinned up a list every day.

The house was old and large. The kitchen and dining room were both in the basement. The whole house was cold, except the kitchen, where there was a large cooking range, and also the sitting room, which had a fire in the grate.

My bed was one of two and measured only two foot six inches wide. I was big by now, so I had a sleepless night, and told Miss Vowles next day.

She was very nice about it, and said she would put me in with two other girls, in a three-foot bed.

So there I stayed for the next three months. I got on well with both girls.

The list was up on my first morning, and two Gladyses were on it. Miss Vowles said, "Oh dear! Which one of you has a second name you would like to be known as here." Mine is Elsie, and so I came to be known by that name.

My first job was to wash the steps outside the entrance, and also the hall floor. This didn't worry me, and I quickly settled in to the routine.

Meals were served to us all on a long table, and they were both good and filling.

Miss Vowles, the cook, and a girl sat at a separate small table. The girl was Miss Vowles' helper, the cleaner of her room, and the one who had complained about her cold bath.

No one seemed to talk to this girl in the sitting room. She was very unusual, but she began to speak to me about her past association with a well-known bandleader, and her singing with his band.

When she went into hospital to have her baby, Miss Vowles asked me to take her place, which I accepted. I found her to be very good with all the different types of girls, and she was very kind to me.

One day she said, "Elsie, how did you get pregnant and homeless?" I told her I wasn't homeless, but I would be going back to my husband after my baby was adopted. She said I was such a sensible girl that she couldn't understand how I had got into such a situation.

One afternoon, she came into our sitting room and said, "Elsie, your husband is on the phone. He wants to meet you."

I went to her room, with her following behind me. It was Ray!

She said I could go out, and so I did, to find Ray in the car outside. I said he mustn't do this, but he said there were things he wanted to say.

He said, "We must part friends, and happily. I don't blame you, but I am just so disappointed that things have turned out as they have."

We drove round and said goodbye and kissed.

Ray was a good kind man, and I knew I was giving up my life's love. It gave me great sadness, yet I still felt it was the right thing to do – and I would have Evelyn.

So I went back to Elm House in a relaxed way. I was grateful my mixed feelings and the dreadful worry and anxiety had been lifted from me.

I kept the position of being Miss Vowles' carer, and no longer sat at the long table. I now sat with Miss Vowles and took round the meals as she served them up. All the girls were friendly, happy and well fed.

I also helped the cook. I would wash up her utensils as she used them, as well as helping a kitchen girl to wash and cut up the vegetables, shredding the cabbage or slicing the onions when we could get any, as they and tomatoes had to be queued for.

The girl who had been Miss Vowles' carer before me was in hospital a long time and came back without her baby. Miss Vowles told me in confidence that she had syphilis and the baby had died. She wasn't back with us very long, and left to live somewhere else.

I used to iron all of Miss Vowles' things, as well as ironing my own when needed.

The weather of winter 1946 was often freezing. The room used by the mothers to bath and feed their babies was very cold, with only a Valor oil stove to give out some heat. No babies died or were ill, but I was very thankful that I still had time for warmer spring-like days before mine was due in May's first week.

Elm House was on the brow of Cotham Hill, and the garden behind was reached by a long flight of stone steps. Miss Vowles used to go down them to tidy up the garden from the winter weather.

One day I asked her if I could help sometime. The first time I did, I slipped and fell down the last few steps, to Miss Vowles' consternation. She said I must see the doctor, but I said I was all right, and luckily I never even had a bruise.

I was so full of fluid that I guess I just bounced, but I never went down those steps again.

We had a religious service every morning and evening, and I played the hymns. I also played pieces on the sitting-room piano, as I still had some of my favourite sheet music in my trunk. I hadn't had a piano to play or to practise on, wherever I had stayed during the war.

The sister from the clinic invited me to come on Saturday afternoons to her parents' home, to play their piano and to have tea with them.

They were an elderly couple. Her father, now retired, made wholemeal bread daily, and grew mustard and cress. The sandwiches made with them were absolutely delicious.

Their piano was old but in tune, and it had an embroidered length of linen covering the entire keyboard. I have never seen another one before or since.

Every Friday Mrs Stott came to tea at Elm House, and afterwards saw 'her girls'. There were about three or four, including myself.

Miss Vowles personally cut and buttered thin slices of bread for her tea. All our rations were pooled, and butter was normally mixed with margarine. I copied this practice right until rationing ceased in the early fifties. Wartime margarine was not like modern margarine, and it tasted horrid on its own.

All our days were busy and active, and we all shared our troubles.

GIs were responsible for many of the pregnancies, and there were a lot stationed in Bristol.

Illegitimate babies were regarded with disgust and shame by most girls' parents, so Elm House was a blessing for them.

Some of the men contributed towards their keep; the Bristol council paid towards destitute cases. Ray paid for me all the time I was there. But we were all a family, all in need, and all cheerful.

One or two of the girls did an outside job after their babies were fostered, until they could get into domestic jobs with their babies.

One of the girls in my bedroom, named Ethel, said that after her baby was adopted she would go and live a long way away, and she intended to forget this period in her life. She was going to have a good life, she said. Her family didn't know she was pregnant and never would.

I had to admire her strong determination – I knew I couldn't be the same.

Children were affecting my whole thoughts as well as my deepest feelings. I now blindly regarded my future life and I considered it my calling to bring up my children to be happy and secure. Marriage was going to be endured with my self-centred, Victorian type of husband. I had lived with him for four years, so I was sure of what lay ahead.

Later, in conversation with Miss Vowles about my future life, I briefly told her that I did not love Rob, and that he was more like a strict brother.

Miss Vowles said, "Elsie, you are thirty, with a lifetime ahead – it is a long time, you know. I do hope everything works out for you."

The words of this single seventy-year-old didn't go deeply. I was thirty, healthy and optimistic. I could cope, I was sure, and I never dwelt on her words. Many years later I knew how wise those words were.

On 30th April at 6.00 a.m. I woke in pain, and, knowing it was labour pains, I got up to ask for an ambulance. I was going to be taken to Southmead Hospital, and I thought it a shame that it wasn't going to be 1st May. The pains were severe and very regular, so I knew it was to be that day.

Miss Vowles saw me out and said, "Elsie, mind it will be a girl – no one wants a boy."

When I arrived at Southmead, an old hospital, all was very busy. A nurse came and said, "All of you on April's last day, we are working flat out!"

She called a doctor, who examined me and told me I was in full labour.

I lay in a room with another mother-to-be, and we were both given gas and air, and one nurse to keep an eye on us. I had never been given any pain relief before, but it did blot out my pain a little.

Suddenly I heard singing outside, and asked what it was – it was certainly lively. I was told it was the cleaning ladies scrubbing the corridor on their knees. They were singing, 'Cruising down the River on a Sunday Afternoon' – the latest song, I was told.

As I was whisked out of the room and into the delivery room, I looked back and saw them both. Their singing continued as my baby was born – a girl weighing almost 8lbs.

I was put on a trolley, with a pad below, and wheeled to the recovery room, where I lay with other mothers from 1 p.m. to 4 p.m. without getting any attention at all.

I began to feel very uncomfortable. I wasn't worried or distressed, I just felt neglected. Eventually I was wheeled into a two-bed ward, and I asked to be washed and changed.

In the next bed was a chatty lady, who had had a son. She told me she came from Wookey Hole and was a farmer's wife, and that the baby's father was an Italian named Carmello. Her husband thought that it was his, after years without success.

I wondered what would happen if the baby grew up to look like an Italian!

The farmer came to see his wife and newborn son. He was a

boring-natured man and his first remark was, "What a poor room! My cowshed looks cleaner than this."

He did have a point, though. It was a dreary, bare-boarded room, with two high beds and no chairs to sit on.

That night I looked down and saw black insects crawling about under my bed. When the nurse brought the night drink, I asked her what they were. She replied, "Oh, cockroaches – they come out at night. They are all right – they don't climb." I had never seen one before, but I took her word and fell asleep.

Next day, Mrs Stott appeared. She wore a navy brimmed hat and a navy two-piece costume, and I remember her kind eyes as she said, "What a lovely baby you have, dear!" and went off. She walked awkwardly – waddled really – and she was always in a hurry.

Later I was told that she rarely had time to come to Southmead, and I should consider myself very honoured. I was also told that, on top of her office duties, she went out often to find the fathers of the girls' babies, in pubs or houses, in order to get their support with money, or, in court cases, to get them to admit paternity.

She was fifty-five, and had a failing mother in her eighties. She lived in a large old house, close to the Gloucestershire cricket ground. She never looked happy or relaxed and I felt sorry for her.

Whilst I was in Southmead, there was an outbreak of a nasty infection amongst the nurses with sickness and diarrhoea, and many went off sick. So all of us suffered from mild neglect, but our babies were brought to us regularly for feeding, and all mothers managed to avoid the debilitating germ.

After ten days in hospital, I went back to Elm House with Ann in my arms. A cot was put beside my bed, and for a fortnight I fed and tended her. Like Evelyn, she was very contented, and only awoke when I needed to feed and bath her.

One afternoon Miss Vowles asked me to go out on an errand for her. I forget why or where I went, but when I came back the cot was empty. I went straight down to see Miss Vowles for the truth of why she had sent me out on this fool's errand.

She said a very nice couple had taken Ann for adoption. They could not have children and would love her. Miss Vowles had told them that I was very musical, and suggested that they should give Ann piano lessons one day.

I had known that I had to give Ann up, but this was so sudden and unexpected.

Next morning the cot, now empty, was still beside me, and I was full of milk. The hospital kept a milk bank, and they came to take it until I could see a doctor.

After tablets were given to me, I became dry, and it was time to make plans to join Rob in London.

He had gone back to work for Mr Lee at Bon Marche in Harlesden, and he had put Michael to live with Ada Cole (Stan Cole's sister) in Neasden. He had written to tell me that he had found rooms with a Mr and Mrs Peacock in Greenford, West London, and if I travelled to Paddington, he would come to meet me there.

Saying goodbye to Miss Vowles, I took a taxi to Temple Meads Station, and alone boarded the train. It arrived at Paddington about half an hour late, and I looked for Rob, expecting his welcome. Instead I found a very cross husband. He told me he had had great difficulty in picking Michael up, along with his luggage, and getting to Paddington on time, only to find that my train was running late!

I asked if we were going to Greenford, and he said, "Of course we are."

Upon arriving at Bridge Avenue, which I found was actually in Hanwell, but right on the border of Greenford, we found a very surprised Mrs Peacock. She said, "I wasn't expecting you today – you didn't tell me; but now you are here, I might as well make up a bed for you."

It was all very bewildering for Michael and myself, as we tried to make ourselves at home, but Rob took it all calmly, as he had got to know the couple well. Next morning he went off to work, taking back Mr Lee's business car.

Bridge Avenue was tree-lined and typically London suburbs. At the bottom of the garden was a large sports field that was used for football, cricket and even archery.

Mrs Peacock (Nelly) soon followed Rob and went off to work also. Her husband, Jack, drove an 'all-nighter' No. 11 bus in London, and was home. He told me they had had a cloudburst and the passageway to the shops, at the side of the sports field, was under water. The River Brent had overflowed and flooded right up to the bottom of their garden.

I was able to use all the kitchen and cooking things, and I found Jack friendly and very cheerful.

When the floodwater subsided, Michael and I walked up to the

Greenford shops, and liked the area very much. The River Brent was pretty and tree-lined, but the water that flowed in it had a muddy appearance. There was a golf course and country all around, and so we settled in fairly quickly.

Michael made friends with the near neighbours' children, all of whom were around the same age, and he went to the local Cuckoo School in Hanwell. It was a pretty rough school, but Mike, as usual, got on with all his classmates.

So there we stayed for the summer and early autumn of 1946.

Rob did his rounds on a bike, until he bought a 1928 Standard 8, with a hood that folded right back to the dicky seat, and running boards on each side of it.

Although it was eighteen years old, it proved to be a reliable little runner, once it started. He found an empty garage to keep it in (belonging to one of his customers), in a road that ran parallel to the River Brent.

After another deluge of rain, the Brent overflowed once again, and Rob and Michael waded through the floodwater to see what damage it had done to our car. Fortunately the water hadn't reached the height of the engine, but once it had subsided, it took a lot of cranking the handle to get the engine running again. Cranking the handle became a regular task for Rob, and many a kick-back resulted in bloodied knuckles for him.

One day a customer told Rob about an empty bungalow in Greenford that was owned by some friends of theirs. The owner was in the civil service. He had been sent to Blackpool along with his family, and the bungalow had stood empty for four years.

The owner wrote to Rob and said, on his friend's recommendation, and because of our homelessness, he would let it to us for four years, after which he expected to return.

We got our home back out of store from Gloucester, and went over daily to clean up a neglected bungalow and our grubby furniture that had been in a dubious Gloucester storeroom since 1944. The inside of the bungalow was very damp and cold, but it slowly took on the look of home.

It was early October when we moved into 47 Eastmead Avenue, but Michael continued going to Cuckoo School, although it was now well over a mile away. He quickly made new friends in the road and still kept his Hanwell friends.

By November, I went to Gloucester to get Evelyn. She was now almost two, and Mrs Pope came to the station to see us off. I promised her I would write, and bring Evelyn back to see her as soon as I could.

Rob's attitude to me now was cold, and at times spiteful. He called me a prostitute, and he spent his evenings with his friends, Stan and Eva, and Eva's parents, Mr and Mrs Collins, all playing solo.

If Evelyn misbehaved, Rob said, "She's Ray's child – what can you expect?"

I became very concerned about her with him, and I had never given a thought to what his attitude towards her might be.

Rob's friend, Stan Cole, called on me one afternoon. I hadn't seen him since 1940. He said, "Tell me, Glad, what is so wrong with you and Rob? He virtually lives at our place!"

I told him we were strangers – not like Eva and himself, so in love and so happy.

He left me in a thoughtful mood. He said, "You two should have stayed apart," and he went.

For Christmas, we all went to my parents. They had invited all the family to come. Some slept on the floor, some shared beds, but we all had a happy time, and both my sisters made a real fuss of Evelyn.

The weather turned cold after Christmas, and it snowed heavily, with deep drifts everywhere. Fuel was no longer being delivered, but you could get coke at the Southall railway yard. We would drive over in the car and queue for a bag every week. It was shovelled into a sack and then weighed, and Rob carried it back to the car.

That bitter winter of 1947 – one of the coldest on record – continued on through February. I had learned from Gloucester how to make good firelighters from newspaper, rolling each page into a tight tube, then tying it into a round. With some sticks, which we kept in the spare room, we managed a fire of sorts. I wouldn't light up until four o'clock each afternoon.

After having gone up to the shops with Evelyn well wrapped up, I put her in Michael's little school chair in front of a poor fire with grey-black coke on top. I said, "Mummy will make you a nice hot drink of tea," and I went out into the kitchen.

Suddenly I heard Evelyn screaming. I rushed in to find her chair tipped over, with her sprawled in the hearth and her hands in the fire. Michael told me she had rocked the little chair backwards and forwards and had tipped over.

I took her next door to the old lady, Mrs Curtis. She grabbed some butter and greased both wrists and hands, and then bandaged them. Her son called a taxi, and Evelyn, Michael and myself sped off to the King Edward Memorial Hospital in West Ealing.

Evelyn was taken into a cubicle and green curtains were drawn around her. A kind doctor said I wasn't to worry as she only had second-degree burns and wouldn't have any scars once they had healed.

After this, life became more and more worrying for me with Rob's ever increasing snide remarks. So one morning I went to the phone box at the top of the road and phoned Mrs Stott. She listened to what I had to say, then told me she would go and see Mr and Mrs Pope. She said she thought that their earlier offer to adopt their granddaughter would probably be the best for Evelyn and for me, as obviously Rob had agreed to take Evelyn without any thought or love for her.

Mr and Mrs Pope agreed at once, and arrangements were made for me to take Evelyn to Elm House. They said they would travel down to Bristol for her.

Snow lay thick everywhere as I arranged for Michael to stay with his new friend's parents at the top of Eastmead Avenue. I had to tell everyone that Evelyn was adopted, and I couldn't keep her. One neighbour told me off well and truly for being selfish. I had to take it all without responding to these cruel criticisms, as it had to look like this for the sake of Rob and Michael.

I still hadn't told Michael the truth about Evelyn, as Rob had insisted he mustn't know. Right from the beginning Michael had never asked and I never told him, but said, "One day I will tell you who she is."

Some three years later, I sat him down and said, "Now I am going to tell you who that little girl was."

Michael immediately responded with, "She's my sister."

"How did you know that?" I asked.

"I've always known," he said. "When I was little I prayed to God for a sister," adding, "I never wanted a brother."

I told Michael that it was to be kept a secret, and that no one must know. That secret was kept, and no one outside our family knew until many decades later.

I returned from Bristol to pick up my life and marriage, and, to the outside world, all looked happy and normal.

To compensate and for company we got Michael a black kitten, which immediately ran off never to return, when the front door was left open. We also bought him a blue budgerigar, which lasted little longer. We found it one morning on the floor of its cage with its feet in the air.

To add to Michael's woes, he was brought home from school one afternoon by his teacher in great pain. During the lunch break, Michael and two of his classmates had gone down to the fields by the River Brent, where apparently gypsies' horses had been tethered. One of his friends had tried to pat one of them and it had lashed out with its hind legs and kicked poor Michael on his right knee. He had unfortunately been standing behind it. His two friends had helped him back to school, whilst he hopped on his one good leg. He endured several days and sleepless nights of pain without complaining.

With the melting of the winter snows and heavy spring rains, flooding was widespread in the Thames Valley.

Rob's father's shack, Otazel, which he now lived permanently in at Walton-on-Thames, right on the banks of the river opposite the weir, had its garden flooded, trapping him. Fortunately it had been built on stilts for such an eventuality, so the interior of the shack remained dry and he was safe.

At the top of Eastmead Avenue were several shops – a grocer's, newsagent's, butcher's, fish and chip shop, and a gents' hairdresser's called Phil's.

Every fortnight or so, Michael had his hair cut there. Phil would place a board over the arms of the chair for Michael to sit on, after having waited perhaps over half an hour for his turn.

I got a job going out cleaning once again, and one Saturday morning, when Michael was with me, he spotted a ginger kitten in the branches of an almond tree in somebody's front garden.

"It's a stray," the lady said. "If you want it, when I can, I'll catch it and bring it along to you."

A few days later, the lady arrived with the ginger kitten in her hands – and so Tigger became a much loved family member for close on ten years.

However, several weeks later, Tigger made a bid for freedom, and for two weeks was nowhere to be found. At night I used to leave the top window of our front room open, and one morning we found him curled up on the settee fast asleep. Tigger had obviously decided that home comforts were far better than the open-road lifestyle.

Tigger was a creamy ginger Persian and had a lovely nature. He never showed his claws or attempted to scratch furniture or people, and he became a wonderful and loving pet.

The lovely summer of 1947 arrived, and life began to look a little brighter for us. Rob had managed to get a council allotment at the top of the road, and on Sunday mornings he would go up there to dig and tend it, growing mainly vegetables.

My walk to the main Greenford Broadway shops was through Ravenor Park. The entrance was close to our bungalow, and at the far end of the park was the library, which Michael and I joined.

I had taught Michael to read at Churchdown, and at the age of four he was able to read and understand many children's books.

When he went to his first proper infant school in Churchdown, he was bitterly disappointed to find himself having to learn, from the beginning, the-cat-sat-on-the-mat-type lessons, which he had passed by over a year before.

Rob was given a week's holiday and he decided we would go to Shanklin on the Isle of Wight. Just before we went I bought a raffle ticket in Greenford Market for a super pedal car. When we got back, an irritated Mr Nelson from next door (No. 49) knocked on our door and said, "Come and get this damn car from our bungalow. It's been blocking up our hallway all the week!"

Michael, now nine, was really too big for it, but pedalled up and down outside and around Ravenor Park in it. Later I advertised it, getting £20. I was then able to buy Michael a small black bicycle, and so his horizons broadened.

One afternoon, a lady called from the Conservative Party, selling raffle tickets, and asked if I had time to put some leaflets through a new council estate's doors. I was so unhappy that I burst into tears. I cried a lot, often after Rob had left for work and Michael was at school.

Mrs Binney asked me to tell her what the trouble was. I couldn't, but said I would be pleased to help her, and this began an association with politics in which Rob joined with me, giving us something we now had in common. We were asked to serve on the local committee, held in the Conservative Hall, and there we met and made friends with a lot of very keen supporters.

The lovely summer of 1947 continued, as did Michael's schooling at Cuckoo School in Hanwell. The long sunny days, with double summer time in operation, often encouraged him to walk the one and a half miles to school.

He kept his Hanwell friends, and, during the summer holidays, on one very hot day, the whole gang of them took sandwiches and bottles of Tizer, as they enjoyed a day out walking to the top of Horsenden Hill.

That August, the funfair arrived for a week in Ravenor Park. Michael was in seventh heaven, spending many hours happily in and around the funfair with its various amusements and exciting pleasure rides. Of course he could only watch for most of the time, but I did take him for a go on the swingboats, whilst Rob took him for a ride on the dodgems. Like Rob, Michael had a good eye and won a packet of five Woodbines on the shooting range, knocking down moving metal ducks.

As with most things, petrol was very much on ration and Rob's expanding credit round meant he didn't have enough petrol coupons to cover the increasing mileage. Of course Rob, as always, knew a man who could get petrol on the black market. He dug a trench in the back garden, where he hid the precious gallon cans of petrol, covering them over with boards and a sheet of tarpaulin.

This enabled us to enjoy a few Sunday trips out to the country or seaside. One particular Sunday we drove down to Shoreham in the Standard 8, which had a top speed of 40 mph, and enjoyed a day on the beach. Coming back home, we chugged up Reigate Hill with ease, passing many broken-down cars with steaming radiators that hadn't been able to make it safely to the top.

Rob's allotment was providing us with fresh produce, and one evening in early September he brought in three freshly cut cobs of corn. I boiled them in a saucepan and served them up on a plate, putting a pat of precious butter on each of them. Michael absolutely adored it and has loved eating it ever since.

With the arrival of the 1947 autumn, Michael along with his Hanwell friends set about knocking ripe mahogany-coloured conkers out of the trees in the long horse-chestnut-lined Cuckoo Avenue, in the centre of the Cuckoo Estate. After threading them on lengths of strong string, conker battles commenced and Michael's proud sixer, having survived six swinging battles, was sadly destined to be smashed into smithereens on the seventh encounter.

On Remembrance Sunday, Rob spent the morning out the front working on his car and, at the appointed hour of eleven o'clock, continued to noisily bang away at his engine whilst Michael and I observed the two minutes' silence. Afterwards I sat down and wrote a letter to the *Middlesex County Times*, which printed it as a leader letter. I wrote that I could not understand how my husband could serve five and a half years in the RAF, where many of his close colleagues had died, yet couldn't stop to mark their memory with just two minutes of his time and silence.

Of course, like everything I said, Rob scoffed and derided my sentiments, saying it was a waste of time and wouldn't bring any of the dead back. I told him the two minutes was for us who were left, to remember the sacrifices they had made for us to live in a free and happier world. My words must have had some sort of influence on him, as each year afterwards the two minutes were solemnly and silently observed.

Michael's tenth birthday was due at the end of November, and I had now taken a job at the Lyons factory in Oldfield Lane on the banks of the Grand Union Canal. I was on the chocolate-cake line and sometimes I was able to bring home damaged cakes. As Michael's birthday neared, I managed to obtain sufficient cakes for his party. He had invited all his friends from Hanwell, but on 27th November a large high-pressure area lay over the British Isles, and by four o'clock in the afternoon, thick pea-soup fog blanketed out all of London and the Home Counties, bringing traffic to a virtual standstill. None of his friends were able to come, as the fog was far too thick for them to attempt the journey from Hanwell, so poor Mike's birthday party was cancelled.

Happily, next year, on his eleventh birthday, all his friends managed to come – the Hanwell gang, his new Clarkes College friends, as well as his Eastmead Avenue pals. This proved to be a turning point for Michael, as after this he quickly lost touch with his Hanwell friends. In future his birthdays would be marked by special treats up in London, like tea in Lyons' Corner House at Marble Arch, or a show or a film in the West End.

1948 was Olympic year and also Michael's eleven-plus year. The various schools he had been to had set him back so much that his form master told me there was no question that he would fail it, and he advised me that private education would benefit Michael if we could afford it.

We took Michael to a private school in Wembley, for an interview with the headmaster in his study. He asked Michael to spell a rather difficult word. I wasn't too sure about it myself, but Michael without hesitation, spelt it out perfectly. We were relieved for him, praising him later back out in the car. However, after much thought and with what we could afford, we decided we would send him to Clarke's College in Ealing, which took boys and girls from the age of eleven to seventeen.

In the early spring of 1948, Rob brought home three Light Sussex hens. He quickly knocked up a henhouse for them, giving them an adequate area to peck and scratch in, and securing it with chicken wire.

They soon became family pets and we named them Faith, Hope and Charity. When they were old enough to start laying, we put a china egg in their laying box to encourage them to lay and were rewarded with freshly laid eggs for the next eighteen months.

Immediately behind us, in Beechwood Avenue, lived the Harlows, who had a pretty little five-year-old daughter called Jean. Mrs Harlow was a hard-working little woman; she went out doing housework and for a short while helped me with my cleaning when I started to develop sinusitis.

Michael would go round to their first-floor maisonette on a Saturday morning to baby-sit with Jean and listen to the omnibus edition of *Dick Barton – Special Agent*, which they both loved listening to on the radio.

The Harlows had a long-haired black cat and he and Tigger became great pals and followed one another around everywhere.

Although Wembley Stadium was little more than three miles away from us, the 1948 London Olympic Games came and went with little or no difference to our daily lives. Rob bought a set of commemorative Olympic stamps for Michael's stamp collection; and in sweltering 90-degrees heat, we did go and watch a runner with a knotted handkerchief on his head, carrying the Olympic flame along the Western Avenue on the day of the opening ceremony. Outside of that, the games continued almost unknowingly to us.

That summer of 1948, Rob's boss, Mr Lee, arranged a firm's outing for all the staff of Bon Marche and their families. He organised a day trip on the paddle steamer *Eagle*, which went from Tower Bridge down the Thames to Southend, then on to Ramsgate. It was an all-day trip and we all met up early at the Tower Pier landing stage on the west side of the famous bridge, before boarding the steamer and settling ourselves inside the main cabin lounge.

We watched fascinated as Tower Bridge rose above us, bringing the traffic to a halt, whilst we steamed underneath and on downstream past the London docks and on towards Greenwich.

Michael ran around the decks happily with the Lees' youngest son, Robin. They went below to the engine room and watched the huge copper-coloured pistons thrusting back and forth, driving the immense round paddles in a kaleidoscopic frenzy of cascading water droplets. They were mesmerised by it.

At Southend, we stopped at the end of the long pier to allow a few of the passengers off, before continuing on out into the open sea and round to Ramsgate, where we all disembarked.

Our stay in Ramsgate was brief – no more than an hour or so – but long enough for us to stretch our legs and enjoy a plate of cockles swimming in vinegar.

The return trip back up the Thames was a happy one, with much laughter and cheery chatter. As we approached Tower Bridge, with the sun sinking in a flame-coloured western sky, they played over the Tannoy system, 'When You Come to the End of a Perfect Day', which for me was the perfect way to end what had been a truly lovely and memorable day.

The week before Michael started at his new school, we spent a week's holiday down at Shoreham at Mr and Mrs Spratt's boarding house, called Holidays. It was timber-built, but large enough for over a dozen guests. It was on the Old Fort Road with the pebbled beach and sea immediately opposite, across the road.

The Spratts, who were in their late sixties or early seventies, had a daughter, Edie, who did all the cooking. Mrs Spratt did the cleaning whilst Mr Spratt waited at the tables and generally saw to all the guests' needs and comforts.

The guest house was happy and friendly with everyone getting on well with one another. One of the guests, a very little boy aged about six, with round-rimmed glasses, came out with a sentence which became a family saying for many a year after. Whilst watching us shrimping at low tide, he suddenly said, "Shrimps are good for little boys –" then, after a pause and a little thought, continued, "and men."

At breakfast time, Mr Spratt would put on the record 'Oh, What a Beautiful Morning!' which was a lovely way to start the day.

Unfortunately one of the breakfasts turned out to be not so beautiful for Michael. Cutting into his sausage, he was horrified to find a large blowfly inside it. Rob called Mr Spratt over to our table and, with profuse apologies, he took the offending sausage and plate away, returning with a freshly fried breakfast for Michael. That evening Mr Spratt told us he had taken the sausage back to his local butcher, who had shrugged his shoulders and said, "It is just one of those things."

Ever after that, Michael would always cut open his sausages before eating them, just to make sure there was nothing unpleasant inside.

At the table next to ours sat a plumpish woman on holiday with her two young daughters. The eldest was a year older than Michael and a keen competitive swimmer who needed to train most days. On one of those days they took Michael with them to the swimming baths in Worthing. This enabled Rob and I to have an afternoon together. So we sat on the beach opposite Holidays with Rob fishing and myself relaxing and enjoying the sunshine and the sound of the sea on the pebbles.

Suddenly Rob's fishing rod bent, and in an instant he was up on his feet and struggling to wind in what proved to be a very large sea bass. We carried it back triumphantly to the guest house, where Edie told us it was a lovely tasting fish. In an effort to make up for the sausage incident, she offered to bake it for us for tomorrow's evening meal. We accepted, and next evening we sat down to eat and enjoy, for the first time, this delicious fish cooked perfectly by Edie.

The following week, Michael started at his new school, Clarkes College, on the New Broadway, Ealing. Although still only ten, and not eleven until the end of November, the school agreed to take him. He dressed in his new purple school blazer and cap, and I took him that first morning on the 97 bus to begin his private education, which we hoped would stand him in good stead for the rest of his life. As I remember, it was £12 a term, which, along with his clothes, sports equipment and books, was not easy to find.

However, a sports shop called George Edwards opened up in a parade of shops at the top of Greenford Broadway. I went along and applied for a position as a shop assistant and got the job. The senior assistant was a friendly and energetic blonde called Doris

Lehay, with whom I quickly formed a close friendship. She was about the same age as me and very fit and sporty, enjoying playing tennis most weekends.

The sports-shop atmosphere was a happy one and I thoroughly enjoyed my days now. Mr Edwards, the boss, hardly ever interfered with our work, and, the few times he was in the shop, he just hovered around in the back stockroom, checking newly delivered items.

Life at home continued fairly well now. Rows still blew up over the most trifling of things, but just as quickly they were forgotten. For all Rob's faults, he never held a grudge and, whatever the row was about, it was soon forgotten and never mentioned again.

A frequent morning cry from Rob was, "I can't find my car keys!" Inevitably he would eventually find them wherever he had last put them down, after having said I must have moved them.

Michael settled into his new school very easily and as usual quickly made friends with several of his classmates. That first day, he came home on the bus with a boy called Peter Bishop and several others who lived in Greenford. Peter was a year older than Michael and destined to become a lifelong friend of his. They were so close that people often thought they were brothers – indeed, I have always looked on Peter as a second son.

Miss Wolfe was a Jewess and Michael's form teacher. She was plump, friendly, and wore thick powder on her face as well as bright red lipstick. She was a good teacher and Michael's education soon showed much improvement under her tutorage.

During the summer of 1949, I wrote to our landlord to ask if we could continue to stay at Eastmead for a further period of time. The owner wrote back to say he was sorry, but he and his family would be returning soon to live there again. So once more we had to think about moving and start looking for another place to live.

Rob took no interest in this situation. I was very worried, but now, quite used to asking for help, I decided to go to see our local councillor, the former Lord Mayor of Ealing, who now sat on the housing committee. I told him the truth: that I had left my husband during the war, but that we had made a fresh life together and now had been given notice to quit our rented bungalow. He didn't give me much hope, but said he would put our name on the housing list.

Appropriate forms were sent to Rob to fill in, but his wages were too high to qualify for a council house or prefab.

We were told, however, that Comben and Wakelin would be building houses at the bottom of Ferrymead Gardens shortly. They would cost £1,750, and we could apply for a building licence to enable us to buy one.

However, a deposit of £150 was needed to acquire one. We didn't have that, so it seemed quite impossible, until one of our Conservative committee said that as Rob had been an RAF volunteer, he could ask the RAF Benevolent Fund to grant a loan. To our relief, they lent us the money. The councillor granted the licence and my father saw to all the legal matters free of charge.

To find out the position of the house we had been allocated, Michael and I walked round to find that the concrete foundations had already been completed and No. 60 was marked on a piece of wood stuck in the ground. Michael told me he knew this plot well, as an air-raid shelter had stood on it and he had played on and around it several times.

To my joy, the semi-detached house would be facing south-east. The kitchen door, which was on the side of the house, faced south-west.

When my father contacted the Land Registry Office, they told him that there was a right of way on the south-west side of our plot, which led on to Ravenor Park.

We definitely didn't want a passageway running alongside us, meaning that our land would have to be split into two plots. My father had to pursue this for us, but it took a year to eventually settle the dispute in our favour.

At the beginning of April 1950, our home went back into store and we moved out of Eastmead Avenue, to find ourselves back in Neasden once again. Rob had talked one of his customers, Mr Sheedy, who lived in Links Road opposite the Welsh Harp, into taking us in on a temporary basis.

Whilst this was happening, Michael went to stay with my mother for a week's holiday. During his stay with her, he bought the first edition of a brand-new comic called the *Eagle*. My mother was concerned that it might be an American 'nasty' comic, but Rob, after scanning it, pronounced it perfectly all right. Michael had this comic delivered to him every week for the next nine years, and still has every one of them – some 450 – in near mint condition.

Whilst we lived at Neasden, Rob took Michael to school in the car, but he had to find his own way home, catching the 83 bus to

Ealing Common, before getting the 112 to Neasden.

Fortunately we were not there long, and before the end of May we were back in Greenford and living with Ricky Richardson and her daughter Sonya, in a first-floor two-bedroom maisonette. Again this was not ideal, as Michael had to share our bedroom again; but at least, with Ferrymead Gardens at the top of the road, we could continue to watch the progress of our house being built.

Ricky was divorced, dark-haired and very attractive. She needed our money in looking after her young daughter, aged six. We all got on well with one another and spent the summer there. I went back to work at George Edwards', whilst all the while our house slowly grew in size. With building materials hard to obtain, progress was much slower than we would have wished.

As August came to an end, Ricky told us that Sonya needed her own room again and we would have to leave. Our house, we had been told, would not be ready for us to move into before November, so we had to look for further temporary accommodation until then.

Doris Lehay at work said she would look after Michael until we were able to move into No. 60. Meanwhile Rob found a room in Perivale, where he and I could stay until then.

From time to time we went up to view the progress of our house, imagining in our minds where our furniture might stand. The damp musty smell of brickwork and cement didn't help to keep our imaginations working for too long, though.

By October, our house looked to be completed, but the foreman told us that it had to dry out before we could move in. Michael came out with the observation that it was incredible that so much time and work had gone into building our house, just for three people to live in. Maybe so, but we were so near now to owning our very first home after fourteen and a half years of unsettled life, and such thoughts were hastily dismissed.

At long last, on 23rd November 1950, we were able to move into our new home and have our furniture and possessions around us once again. Of course there were many things we needed, but these came gradually as and when we could afford them. Rob's boss, Mr Lee, kindly gave us a huge pre-war Kelvinator refrigerator, which we were very pleased to accept.

The hall, lounge and dining room all had parquet flooring, and in the lounge, built to our specification, was a lovely red-brick fireplace. The dining room had a single-door French window that led out into the back garden. Upstairs were three bedrooms, a bathroom and separate toilet. Rob and I slept in the large front bedroom, whilst Michael had the small front one. The third back bedroom was the spare room.

Our garden, such as it was, was a nightmare. The builders had left behind broken bricks and building rubble of all sorts, which Rob was still digging up several years later.

So our new life at 60 Ferrymead Gardens began. Those weakest of roots, which we had put down in Greenford in late 1946, looked to have now matured into a strong and binding root for all three of us.

I was content that Evelyn, now almost six, was being brought up in Hucclecote in a far happier atmosphere than she would have had with Rob. As for Ann, now called Jennifer by her adoptive parents – well, they wanted no further contact with me, so I could only hope that she was happy too.

The rows continued, however, as did Rob's ever lengthening working hours. Michael continued his schooling at Ealing and I made friends with the new neighbours around me. I was now thirty-six, and although I didn't know it then, I had over fifty years of my life still ahead of me. Some of these years would be happy and some of them very unhappy. We would make twelve further moves to the counties of Hampshire, Kent, Sussex and finally Devon. Along the way, we experienced a failed business where we lost almost half of our capital, a nomadic existence in the mid 1960s, a severe cerebral stroke in 1982 and much much more.